Creating Your New Lifestyle

Creating Your New Lifestyle

Change Your Behaviors and Succeed on any Diet

Hamilton C. Erridge

Creating Your New Lifestyle

First printing 2007

Cover Design, Interior Design, and Printing by

Falcon Books, San Ramon, California

ISBN 10: 0-9793455-0-2
ISBN 13: 978-0-9793455-0-0

Library of Congress Catalogue Number: 2007922189

Published by

Online System Innovations

2415 San Ramon Valley Blvd., Suite 4-301
San Ramon CA 94583

10 9 8 7 6 5 4 3 2 1

PRINTED IN THE UNITED STATES OF AMERICA

To my wife Adina—

For her continued love and support.

. . . .

To my friend Robb—

For not only believing in the mission of this book, but proving it each day by reporting to cubicle 1411e. Something no one should ever be asked to do.

. . . .

To my friends on "the board"—

For proving each day that when we help others, we are truly helping ourselves.

Contents

Introduction

Welcome to Your New Lifestyle

It seems like just yesterday, I decided that I had reached my limit. I was tired of being overweight, tired of wearing clothes that didn't fit, tired of the way people looked at me, and tired of not having control over my eating. I'm not sure how it happened, but I suddenly had the realization that I was 100 pounds overweight and I did not want to continue living my life this way.

As someone who has been on just about every commercial diet, I simply did not have the energy or enthusiasm to go on another program with pre-packaged foods and weekly visits with people that had no idea of the eating issues that I faced. Sure, they were nice people and seemed well-intentioned, but I wanted something that would work, and work fast. Let's face it; I knew that I needed to lose 100 pounds, and even under the best circumstances, losing that much weight would take me probably a year on most programs. For me, my weight issues were directly related to my relationship with food. In fact, I had such a great relationship, that I seemed to always be eating. Food had somehow taken over my life and I no longer had control.

I needed a solution that would allow me to take a break from food, allow me to lose the weight, and allow me to begin living a new life. Unfortunately, that solution did not exist. So, with few choices, I was forced to get assistance from a large commercial diet program that offered little support, little understanding, and no empathy for what was really going on with me. Sure, their brochures said they offered all kinds of support, but in reality, unless you have been or are a large person, and faced the day-to-day issues, it's an issue that is almost impossible to understand.

Now, this is not to say that many wonderful medical professionals are not concerned about their patients' well-being, but simply, they don't understand that losing weight and maintaining the weight loss has less to do with food, and more to do with the reasons behind the eating. So, in choosing a diet, I quickly came to the realization that while my doctor could offer me advice on the right caloric formulas to follow and the biochemistry of what was going on with my body, he simply could not offer me what I really needed—the true understanding behind my eating and the necessary skills for keeping the weight off. Fortunately, I was able to recognize this early on and with no other options available to me, I learned to keep my mouth shut and not press the issue. But it didn't take long to realize that while I could lose weight, the real demons that I faced were still around.

The fact is that while I was losing weight, I was painfully aware that I was not overcoming the hard issues. And, in knowing that, it became clear that unless I was able to overcome these issues, I was destined to repeat the past and put the weight back on. What made matters even worse was that I felt totally alone in what I was facing.

Clearly, my doctor did not understand me, and my wife, who did not have a weight issue, did not understand me either. As anyone with a weight issue knows, it can often feel like you are on your own island of eating insanity. In fact, I came to believe that I was the only one in the world that had these feelings or acted in crazy ways when it came to food. For example:

- If ice cream was in the fridge and I didn't want my wife to know that I had eaten some, I would carefully remove only the top layer.
- If my wife did any sort of baking and I discovered the plate of goodies, I would immediately take as much as I thought I could without it being noticed on the plate. And I would even go so far as to rearrange the items, to make it appear that none had been taken.
- When sitting on the couch, I would always hold a pillow in my lap. This way, I could pretend that my belly didn't exist.
- At work, my morning break would usually consist of what most people eat for lunch. Then, at lunch, when going out with co-workers, I would claim that I wasn't that hungry. It was as if I had gotten overweight from some sort of external factor that was out of my control. Surely, since I didn't eat that much (in public), it wasn't from overeating.
- No trip in the car was complete without food by my side. So, when going on any sort of errand, provisions were always necessary. Whether it meant going through a drive-through for fast food, or grabbing something at the check-out counter, driving never ceased to offer the lethal eating combination of privacy and convenience for eating.
- I used to ride on a train to get to work and this was what I would consider my secret snacking time. Basically, before getting on the train, I would pick up some candy, and then when riding, I would try and put the candy in my mouth without anyone noticing. I was a Secret Candy Agent on an

almost daily commute mission to see what could be consumed without anyone noticing.

- Going to the grocery store meant only one thing—eating while shopping. Surely, I couldn't be expected to buy the food without trying it first! So, as I would enter the grocery store, I would immediately open up a bag of something and munch on it as I cruised around. And no trip to the grocery store was complete without having to arrange something in the bag for the trip home. Yes, it was only three blocks, but how could I survive without something to munch on? In fact, it got so bad that I would arrange the items on the checkout cart so that my "on the way home survival food" would be strategically placed on the top of the bag. Of course, what really was bad about this was that my wife thought I was the most helpful guy in the world. Always more than pleased to go to the grocery store to pick something up, without her knowing the true nature of my grocery store missions.

- No matter what the charity event, everyone in our neighborhood knew that whether they were selling candy or cookie dough, I was definitely their primary customer. And, upon buying it, I would always say, "But it's for a good cause...I didn't buy it for me, I bought it to help the kids, school, etc."

- Vacations were not about enjoying the trip, but about the new and exciting foods that had yet to be discovered and eaten.

- Going on a business trip only meant one thing...full access to the mini bar. And they restock it each day!! Of course, I would then have to explain why I had a $300 dollar mini bar tab on my expense sheet. Funny, but the excuse that I was entertaining clients only seemed to work once.

- "Leftovers" in our house was really just code for...wait until my wife goes to sleep, then polish off the evidence.
- When clothes became tight, this was not a sign that it was time to start a diet, but a sign that it was time to buy bigger clothes.
- When cooking, I always bought extra food to ensure that during the critical taste testing process, I would have plenty to taste while cooking, and plenty left over for eating when done.
- Elastic waistbands were not made for large people; they were made for people who were so active, they needed pants to stretch with them.
- When buying take-out food, I would often ask for several sets of forks, napkins, sodas, or an extra sandwich, or any number of other stupid things to make it appear that I was ordering for more then one person. Of course, I wouldn't want anyone to think that I was buying all of that food for myself. And, of course, this would only lead to eating the evidence...a vicious cycle!
- Moving from Large to XL to XXL to XXXL was a sign of progress that should be rewarded with going out to dinner.
- Feeling hungry and tired was not just a temporary state of mind, but a constant existence. However, to fight this problem, I would rely on coffee and candy throughout the day for energy—a slippery slope that only further exacerbated the problem.

And my own personal list went on and on. Now, I'm not suggesting that every overweight person has the same sort of issues that I did in my own life, but it's a fairly well known fact that most people use food to comfort themselves or to handle stress. In a way, it's become our modern day drug of choice for handling discomfort and providing a moment of caloric bliss when faced with stress of family or work. And, if anyone knows about this, I do. In fact, I think it's safe to say that I was once the poster child for comfort and stress eating. Unfortunately, overeating is one of those problems that we literally wear on our bodies. Unlike someone with a drug or alcohol issue, when you are a larger person, people know it the moment that they see you. And, in my case, the more that I used food for various reasons in my life, the more obvious it became with each pound that I put on. Of course, like anyone with a problem that they don't want to admit or aren't ready to deal with, I had a huge list of excuses for not only my eating, but for the evidence that was often left behind, including:

> "The guys at work today left their lunch bags in the car."
>
> "The candy wrappers are from the free samples being handed out at the grocery store."
>
> "I told the guys to take their chips with them, but I guess they forgot."

Amazingly, the more I would say these sorts of things, the easier it became to actually believe them. Then, you wake up one day, look in the mirror and realize that denial is not a river in Egypt, but the way that you have been living your life.

So, if you're feeling like you are a little out of control, please know that you are not alone. I once faced the same issues and I understand what you are going through. And if someone like me was able to overcome these issues and learn to develop new behaviors in my life, then anyone can do it.

As per my own story, I would like to say it started with my weight loss, but the true adventure did not begin until a very sleepy afternoon in 2002 when I decided to start a discussion board on the internet to talk about my own weight loss and the issues that I was facing. And, for the most part, having no idea what I was doing, I spent a few days writing my thoughts in various posts. I didn't have any systematic approach to what I was doing, but just being able to write my thoughts down seemed to provide some peace of mind for the first time in my life.

But, not surprisingly, I soon became tired of writing and I lost interest. I also thought that no one was reading. Remember, this was just a discussion board that I created for fun and while it was accessible to anyone on the internet, I didn't really have any marketing behind it. So, after about a week, I stopped writing and found myself back in my own private world of my own eating issues that no one around me could really understand.

A couple of weeks passed, and then, a very amazing thing happened—I received an e-mail from someone asking me why I had stopped writing. And, to my amazement, upon returning to the discussion board, I found that several hundred people had begun posting and discussing their individual eating issues and the challenges that they were facing.

So, in seeing other people posting about the same feelings and thoughts, I can honestly say that for the first time in my life, I did not feel so alone. Or I was at least not the only crazy person in the world. Either way, it was great to discover that I was in good company and that the issues that I was facing were shared by people not only in the United States, but by people in every country in the world. And, regardless of where they were from, we shared the same thoughts and issues, and often lacked understanding from family, friends, or physicians. Consequently, for the first time, I found that I was not alone and before my very eyes I had somehow created a unique community where hard to discuss issues could be openly talked about in a supportive and understanding manner.

So, I continued to develop the discussion board and literally talked with thousands of other people about their own issues and challenges. And, in doing so, I came to the realization that while many different options exist for dieting, every dieter faces the same universal set of challenges. And, unless these issues are dealt with, managed, and overcome, the person dieting is destined to repeat the past—no matter how successful they were on their diet.

Like most people, when I originally thought about losing weight, all I really wanted to do was figure out a way that I could lose the most amount of weight, in the shortest amount of time. My entire focus was on the end goal, with very little thought on why I had put on the weight to begin with, or what was stopping me from putting it back on when I had lost it all.

With this determination and focus on the end goal, I continued dieting and eventually reached my goal of losing 100 pounds. I proved that it could be done!!! However, with very little guidance, I did it through the school of hard knocks. And, when I reached my goal, I realized that while I had successfully lost the weight, I should have also been preparing for my new life ahead. Sure, I had some handouts to read and I had a few discussions about this with my doctor, but to truly prepare oneself for maintaining the weight afterwards takes much more. Basically, it takes coming to terms with one's own issues, facing these behaviors head-on, and learning how to create a new lifestyle!

Over the next 5 years, I analyzed my own thoughts and behaviors, and began documenting the challenges of others on the board. And, in doing so, I not only successfully addressed my own issues, but was able to create a set of thoughts and approaches that would allow others to overcome their own eating and weight loss issues. To put the program to the test, I founded the New Lifestyle Diet. Not surprisingly, when people applied these principles along with a healthy weight loss program, the results were incredible. In fact, the New Lifestyle Diet has now gone on to help thousands of people lose weight, get control of their issues, and change their lives forever. However, I didn't start the discussion board or the diet as businesses, I created them as mechanisms to allow people to come together and overcome the same issues. So, with that same sprit, I decided to write this book. Being someone who has lived with the issues of overeating and being overweight, I know how hard life can be. So, I wrote this book with one simple goal in mind—to allow anyone on any diet the opportunity to gain control, create new skills and behaviors, and learn to keep the weight off for the rest of their life.

I'm very proud to say that within this book are not only my own experiences and observations, but also very valuable personal lessons that are located at the end of each chapter. These lessons are presented to you in the shape of *Personal Ingredients* that will provide you with various opportunities to think about the issues in your own life and provide you with skills that you can begin using immediately. As you progress, it's important to remember that the process of creating a new lifestyle is much like the process of preparing your favorite recipe. While each ingredient that you add to a recipe requires preparation, when you put them all together, they create the perfect balance. As a result, as you progress through the book and work through the Personal Ingredient included with each chapter, you'll learn a little bit about yourself and develop the skills for overcoming past behaviors and developing new ones that are critical to long-term weight loss success. Then, as you go about your life and encounter different challenges or recipes along the way, you'll be equipped with your personal ingredients list and ready to take on any challenge.

I have no doubt this book will bring you inspiration, laughter, and the thoughts and knowledge to truly create a new and healthy lifestyle. While some things may seem awful and others hilarious, the insight, inspiration, approaches, and new behaviors that you'll develop are all put together to ensure your success. It's amazing, but as you progress on your journey, you'll look back on the overall experience and remember the little things the most. Yes, reaching your goal weight is an exciting event, but it's the things that most people take for granted that will stand out the most to you, including:

- Shopping for clothes and not having to enter a store and wonder if they carry your size.
- Having strangers smile at you for no reason at all.
- Having people take you seriously and not pre-judge you by the way you look.
- Actually wanting to have your photo taken.
- No longer viewing your clothes or hair as a vehicle for hiding your body, but as a vehicle for showing it off.
- Viewing exercise as not something that you have to do, but as something that you enjoy and truly look forward to each day.
- No longer feeling self-conscious about eating in public or ordering food.
- No longer sweating or feeling hot all the time.
- Discovering that the medication you are taking today may not be necessary when you've lost the weight.
- Discovering the amazing feeling that you aren't hungry 24/7.

- Taking back control from those around you and no longer feeling that you are being taken for granted due to your size.
- Being attractive to your spouse and having them look at you like they did when you first met.
- Looking forward to traveling again and no longer fearing the looks of strangers as you board a plane looking for your seat.
- Getting back in touch with your body and learning to appreciate the look and feel of it.
- Taking back control of your eating, instead of being at the mercy of your cravings and the temptations around you.
- Feeling proud of your accomplishment and being seen by your kids, friends, and family as a role model.
- Giving yourself a new lease on life and beginning to live life to its fullest.
- Being inspired to take on new challenges and accomplish goals you never thought possible.
- No longer going to the doctor and being embarrassed or dreading the impending weight conversations that you know are going to come up each time.
- Being able to put on clothes and feel sexy.
- Waking up each morning and feeling good about being in control of your body and your eating.
- Looking in the mirror each day and truly enjoying the reflection that is looking back at you.

These are just a few examples of the things in your life that are going to change. But let me assure you, the list is infinite! So, what I really want to impress upon you is that if you are not already excited about what it is you are doing for yourself and how your life is going to change, then start smiling—because you have a very exciting life ahead of you.

Creating a New Lifestyle isn't something that happens quickly. It is a gradual and evolutionary process that involves slowly changing your behaviors and mindset. During the course of your weight loss, you'll go through a number of different changes. The biggest change is being at peace with yourself and the ongoing personal journey of development and modification. And, while the physical weight loss was your initial motivation for change, you'll come to realize that the true nature of change comes from the new habits and lifestyle that you are developing. Ultimately, to succeed, you'll learn to leave behind the old habits that allowed you to become overweight and develop new habits that will allow you to enjoy a healthy fit body for the rest of your life. As you can imagine, implementing these new behaviors is not easy, and it's not uncommon for most people to feel a little panicky as they begin the diet. However, once you discover that you can successfully apply new changes, you'll feel a fresh sense of empowerment. You'll not only start to feel better as a result of your weight loss, but you'll also find yourself becoming more excited about the future ahead of you.

If you are like most people, you'll be a little anxious or have negative thoughts with regards to the process of creating change in your life—especially as it relates to weight loss. For example, have you ever found yourself saying, "What is going to be different about this diet from all the rest?" Or "I've failed so many times before, why is now any different?" The answers to these questions are simple. For the first time in your life, you are going to take responsibility for the behaviors that you've already developed, and for the actions that are required to overcome them.

Losing weight is not just about eating less. It's about getting to the root of the issues, truly addressing the actions that are causing you to be overweight, and putting together the necessary steps to allow you to live a new and healthy lifestyle. What is often intimidating about taking responsibility is that most people believe they don't have the necessary skills, knowledge, or drive to successfully lose weight or keep it off. But, by the very act of reading this book, you've already proven that you have the drive and the desire to change.

So, as you read this book, keep in mind that the book has been designed to address many topics that are to be read and thought about individually. And, while each chapter focuses on a new subject, the contents within them can be read cover-to-cover, or enjoyed one at a time. Regardless of how you choose to read the book, take the time to think about the issues being discussed and enjoy the journey. And, as you progress, you'll soon find yourself with the skills to not only reach your goal weight, but to be in control and have the confidence that you can live your life free of your eating and weight issues.

Now, if you're ready...let's create your New Lifestyle!!

Sincerely,

Hamilton C. Erridge

Chapter One

Choosing Your Path

"The greater thing in this world is not so much where we stand as in what direction we are going."

— Oliver Wendell Holmes

One of the most confusing things about dieting is determining which diet is the right one for you. And, unless you have been hiding under a rock, you already know that literally hundreds of different diets exist. In fact, in choosing a diet, the entire process can be extremely overwhelming and stressful. Not only are we faced with the issues of losing the weight and keeping it off, but at the same time, we are required to make a choice on choosing the best path. Obviously, we don't want to make a mistake, so we then turn to our most trusted sources—family, friends, physicians, television, magazines, and the internet. And, although it might seem obvious, this is where we all make our first mistake.

Fundamentally speaking, what everyone does wrong is to approach weight loss with the goal of getting the weight off. And, in choosing a diet, everything considered revolves around the speed and process of losing the weight. In doing this, the biggest factor for success is ignored. That is, the issues that caused a person to become overweight in the first place. As with most ailments that we face, being overweight is no different: the symptom is treated, but the underlying cause is ignored.

Any diet is really just a tool and a process for losing weight. And, like a carpenter who is starting a job and has to choose the best tool to use, you also have to choose the right diet or program for taking the weight off. In facing this decision, don't think solely in terms of which diet will help you to lose weight, but focus on your issues and the steps that you must take to overcome them at the same time. So, by the time you reach your goal weight, the new person on the outside has also taken significant steps to make changes on the inside.

In choosing the best path and diet for you, begin by asking yourself the following questions:

- How much weight do you have to lose? Is it 10 to 20 pounds, 20 to 50 pounds, 50 to 100 pounds, 100 to 200 pounds, 200 to 300, or more?
- Have you put on weight because you haven't been exercising or eating in a healthy manner?
- Have you put on weight because food has always had more control over you than you've had over it?
- Have you started and stopped diets countless times?
- Do you find yourself eating as a result of stress or a need for comfort?
- Do you find yourself eating as a result of sadness or loneliness?
- Do you find yourself eating as a result of social or family pressures?
- Do you find yourself eating as a result of boredom or for entertainment?

Please know that in asking yourself these questions, you may very well not know the answers. In fact, for many of you, this might be the first time in your life that you have been asked to think in this sort of manner.

Whatever your background, there are those who have lifelong issues with food: where food has always controlled them; where food is used as a way of comforting oneself and handling stress; where temptations and cravings are a constant battle. And, there are those who have put on weight over the years because of a change in lifestyle, career, kids, bad eating habits, and overall lack of exercise. And there are those that share traits from both groups. But what matters most is that regardless of the amount of weight you have to lose, the most important thing is your own issues in relation to food and what it is you are trying to correct.

So, in approaching the different diets that are available, you want to consider whether the diets that you are looking at will not only allow you to lose the weight, but more importantly address the very issues that you are trying to overcome.

If you are someone who has simply developed bad eating habits over the years and does not have inherent issues with food, then the chances are that you'll do well on just about any commercially available weight loss program. However, if you are someone who is trying to overcome lifelong issues with food, then you'll need to be more selective. You'll need to find a program that will allow you to step away from food in a safe and healthy manner, lose the weight, and then re-approach the relationship from a healthier perspective.

Losing the weight is the easy part; coming to terms with your own behaviors and truly addressing and changing them is where the majority of your focus needs to be. But if you are on the wrong diet and are faced with too many choices or foods, losing the weight is going to be nearly impossible. Of course, this all comes down to the individual.

In writing this book, I did it from the perspective of providing anyone on any diet the ability to overcome their own issues and get control of their eating. Ultimately, we all have different backgrounds and challenges to overcome, and when it comes to losing weight, not all diets will address the likes and dislikes of each person. However, what is fantastic is that the challenges are universal and the principles in this book will allow anyone to be successful. So, what matters most for you right now is not how you are going to lose the weight, but more importantly, to determine the issues that you want to overcome along the way. And, for those that aren't sure of what they are, have no fear. In reading the book, you'll be faced with questions and funny situations that you'll laugh about along the way and through which you'll come to recognize your own issues. And, amazingly, you'll even learn to develop strategies for overcoming them.

. . . .

A Simple, Yet Very Hard Question

If you are someone who went for years ignoring your weight gain and not doing anything about it, can you think of a reason why it took you so long to attack the issue? Or, in simpler terms, why did you wait so long to do something about your weight problem?

As insensitive or lacking in understanding as this question may seem, this is actually something that my wife asked me a few years ago. Of course, what makes it so funny coming from her is that she is someone who has never had a weight problem and cannot even remotely understand what it's like to overeat on a continuous basis or use food to handle stress or cravings. Now, what she meant by her inquiry is actually very specific. Allow me to explain: From the perspective of someone who doesn't have a weight problem or any eating issues, she treats her own weight as something that needs to be handled from time-to-time. Meaning, if she puts on a few pounds and feels that her clothes are getting tight, she simply cuts back on her eating. So, in viewing the world from her perspective, it's literally impossible for her to understand how I could have put on 100 pounds over an extended period of time without ever stopping along the way to do something about it. The question really has nothing to do with a single event in my life or a call to action, but it's more related to why I didn't stop the insanity along the way. Why did I choose to ignore the problem and allow the weight to build up over time?

And it is this simple question that really allowed me to get to know myself better. It allowed me to come to terms with the understanding that I wasn't necessarily ignoring the problem, but more that I was ignoring the causes. Meaning, I personally used food to handle stress and to comfort myself. And it wasn't until I was able to get a grasp on these concepts that I even had a chance at losing the weight and keeping it off. In addition, what makes having these issues truly unique is that as an overweight person, we all literally carry our issues with us. So, when I had reached the point of being 100 pounds overweight, it was my own personal breaking point of knowing that things had become out of control and that I needed to figure out what was going on. In fact, what was truly funny about the process is that I started losing weight without even having a clue as to what was going on in my life to cause me to be overeating so much. But, like two worlds that almost immediately collide, the act of dieting and the need to comfort myself had very little room for one another. So, it was with great pain that I was able to come to terms with my own issues and carry on. However, do not think for a moment that my issues or your issues are so black and white.

Meaning, they are often shades of grey, including overeating, comforting ourselves, dealing with unhappiness, and an overall lack or non-existence of exercise. In fact, this question is often the easiest to answer for those that do have identified problems (stress or comfort eating). However, for those that have not come to terms with their own issues yet or truly put on weight because of bad eating habits or a love of food, this question can be incredibly difficult. In many ways, whether you have issues or not, the truth is still the same. We all put on weight over an extended period of time, watched it happen in the mirror and did nothing about it. To an outsider, it can all seem very crazy. But, to those reading this and having lived this experience, it's a very real thing and can also be equally confusing with hindsight. But in working through this puzzle, it is also one of the biggest steps forward that you can make towards your own understanding of yourself and long-term success.

. . . .

Get Busy Living or Get Busy Dying

Just like in the movie Shawshank Redemption, we each have to look at ourselves in the mirror and ask the question, do we choose to get busy living, or get busy dying? And if the answer is dying, then we choose to roll over and accept the feelings, discomfort and the isolation of being overweight. But if we choose living, then we choose to move forward and lose the weight and take on the battle. We decide to take back our lives, to fight for our own happiness, and to truly live life to its fullest again. But, the choice belongs to you.

. . . .

If Not Now, When?

Anyone on a diet knows that the process of being disciplined and learning how to control your eating will test every ounce of strength that you have. It will test your will power, your sense of humor, your discipline, and ultimately—it will test how badly you want to change your life.

Remember, we all started our diets to change our lives, so ultimately, our success or failure comes down to how badly we make this diet the number one priority in our life. For many of us, we find ourselves with a lifetime of putting others' needs in front of our own. Now is the time to put your needs first. Now is the time to be a little selfish and follow the diet 100%. Sure, it may be uncomfortable for you and those around you, but now is the time for change.

What is really exciting about the process of losing weight is that it presents the unique opportunity to take a stand, face your eating issues head-on, and start living your life to its fullest. I know for me, I put my life on hold for far too long until I found the strength to ask myself the question...If not now, when?

And, for me...The answer was simple. NOW IS THE TIME!!!

So, if you really want to be successful, all you have to do is follow your diet. Not on a part-time basis, not when things are going well, but 100% all of the time. Take this moment and decide that you will have the conviction to go for it and see this diet through until you have reached your goal weight. Promise yourself that now is the time for change and that nothing is going to stop you from achieving this goal.

For me, my diet presented a final opportunity to make up for past starts and stops, an opportunity to really suck it up and do it for real. No more excuses!!

Make the promise to yourself right now that you are not going to let anything stop you from being successful. Own the responsibility of it and create your own destiny!! I know it might sound funny, but if you don't take control now and make this the time in your life for change, when will you do it?

Personal Ingredient I: Creating Your Attack Plan

The first ingredient towards your new lifestyle starts with having the ability to identify the behaviors that are impacting your eating and your resulting weight. Remember, most people go on a diet, lose the weight and then put the weight back on. Having the ability to lose weight proves that the dieter has the discipline to stick with a diet. Unfortunately regaining the weight also indicates that the dieter was unsuccessful in identifying or resolving underlying issues of eating. As a result, the first and most important personal ingredient addresses the need to identify your own behaviors and begin the process of putting an action plan in place for allowing you to overcome them.

To start this process, take a moment and think about the following 5 questions:

What do you want to change about yourself?

When you think about this question, think in terms of the little things that you do on a daily basis, that have a direct impact on your weight. Some of these things could be the habit of starting your day with a muffin or a donut, skipping breakfast, stopping for fast food on your way to or from work, eating while shopping on your way home from the grocery store, eating unhealthy lunches or dinners, eating the kids' snacks, having ice cream at night, or finding that your cravings have more control over you, than you have over them. The list goes on and on, and is as diverse and unique as each person. The important things to think about are your own personal behaviors and the things that you would like to get under control. Now, don't feel bad if you start to think about your own list and the issues seem infinite. I know for myself, when I went through this process, my own personal list was over 50 items long. What matters most right now is taking the time to think about the behaviors that you want to overcome. So, take a moment, pull out a piece of paper and make your own personal list. While doing this might seem a little intimidating, know that the personal behavior list that you are creating is actually the start of your own attack plan for taking back your life and truly creating a new lifestyle.

What are your personal triggers?

While your behavior list may seem long and intimidating, the events or circumstances in our lives that lead to our behaviors are often very similar. Meaning, the majority of people seek comfort in food to handle stress or anxiety. Often, they aren't hungry at all, but are simply seeking a few moments of caloric solace in their day. For example, whenever I had a stressful meeting at work or got into an argument with my wife, I would immediately find myself reaching out for food. For some, certain people or situations in their lives can trigger a response or a desire to eat. What really matters most is trying to identify various events in your life that you associate with your poor eating behaviors. In doing this, you'll find that regardless of how big your list of behaviors is, certain events in your life will stand out more and more. And you'll start to understand yourself a little better.

Is food helping or hurting you?

In examining your own behaviors and the events that cause them, the next step is to examine the consequences that you would like to change. For example, if you are someone who eats because of stress or anxiety, does the food make you feel better? When you get into an argument with a family member, does food help to resolve the stress? Regardless of the behaviors that you are trying to overcome, begin to think about the things that food is providing for you and what it represents to you. For some people, it's not so much about emotion, but more about situation. Food has become such a huge part of celebrating and being social that it's hard to enjoy the company of others without having any event surrounded by eating. In examining your own behaviors, think about the consequences of what it is you are trying to overcome.

What are your personal goals?

While it's impossible to overcome all of your behaviors at one time, it's critical to have goals and an action plan for allowing you to take baby steps along your journey. So, for each of the behaviors that you are trying to overcome, create clear and concise goals for overcoming them. Some examples include:

"I will no longer eat in my car."

"I will no longer visit the vending machine at work."

"I will no longer eat fast food."

"I will no longer eat late at night."

"I will no longer drink mocha lattes."

For each one of your behaviors, try and come up with a clear goal. Keep in mind that this is not an easy thing to do. For the first time in your life, you may be admitting to things that you would rather not be thinking about. Write them down on paper. This is a personal exercise just for you and is for your eyes only.

Then, having completed your list of goals, take the time to list out an action plan. For example, when I feel stressed, I will go outside and get some fresh air, instead of visiting the vending machine. When I'm out with friends and we order our mocha lattes, I will order a nonfat latte or have bottled water. Or, since I've gotten into the bad habit of eating fast food on my way home each night, I'll take another way home so that I won't be tempted. Having this action plan is critical! As you can see, in listing out each of your behaviors, and listing your goals with an action plan for each, you have now given yourself a plan of attack for creating your new lifestyle. So now no matter what situation you face, by taking the time to think about the behaviors that you are trying to overcome and the actions that you will take when faced with them, you now have a working model. Definitely don't discount the power of having your plan to help in overcoming any challenge that you face.

How will you reward yourself?

This might seem silly, but taking the time to celebrate your small victories along the way is critical. Creating your new lifestyle isn't just about the score on the scale, but it's about the little victories along the way and being able to overcome the challenges that you face on a day-to-day basis. Take the time to reward yourself. For example, after you have achieved a small victory, you might reward yourself by ending the day with a bubble bath, taking a moment and smiling in the mirror, or looking over your list and putting a check mark next to the behavior that you were able to overcome. I know for myself, my own personal list was infinite, but with each small success that I had, I always took the time to check off my behavior list and remind myself that I was slowly facing down each of the behaviors in my life that had been holding me back.

Taking the time to identify your behaviors, the events, the consequences, and having clear goals and an action plan will allow you to have the framework for a working plan to take back your life. Then, always reward yourself along the way; it will help to keep the journey fun, and also serve as a reminder that although the ingredients for success are small, each one of them is taking you one step closer to your new lifestyle.

Chapter Two

The Power of Goals and Motivation

"Obstacles are those frightful things you see when you take your eyes off your goal."

— Henry Ford

The challenge to being successful when dieting is finding your individual motivation. For me, the diet was all about achieving a goal that has been accomplished by very few people. At one point in my life I had aspirations of playing professional sports, but life seemed to have other plans for me. In fact, after college, I soon found myself in a career, then marriage, then a mortgage. And, to make matters even more complex, I was 100 pounds overweight. Whose life was this? It certainly wasn't the one I had originally planned. Of course, for the most part, everything was great, but to get things back on course, the weight had to first come off.

First I came to terms with my own sad reality... that I was too old to ever play professional sports. Despite this fact, I could at least treat my diet as my own pro challenge. Sure, it wouldn't be the same as playing ball in front of 45,000 people, but just like football, if it were easy, everyone would be doing it.

From my perspective, losing weight is for those that have a fire burning inside of them and a desire to change their life. To no longer accept their circumstances, to stand up, and shout from the roof tops that they want to lose the weight, get fit, and take back their life! Do you have that fire? If so, then go for it!!!

When I started, I didn't know where the journey would take me, but I had faith in that I was willing to change my life and that when I came out the other side, the results would go far beyond just weight loss. And the fact is, I was right. The results of losing the weight completely changed my life and I'm extremely passionate about others having the same experience. I cannot stress this enough. Take on the challenge of losing weight and simply own it...stick with it and reap the benefits!!

For those of you who might be down or depressed because of your size or feeling like your eating is out of control, try seeing the act of losing weight as a personal test. It's the moment in time that determines if you have what it takes to separate yourself from the rest of the pack. This is your opportunity to do something that most people cannot do. This is your opportunity to show yourself just how much you can accomplish.

While you have no way of understanding what I'm talking about until you reach your goal weight, please trust me on this...Do whatever you can to reach it!!! The new feeling and outlook that you get on life is something that will change you forever.

Personally, I cannot think of anything that you can possibly eat that can replace all of what I'm talking about. Please take the challenge and continue on the path. I promise you the results will be far greater then you could ever imagine.

. . . .

Time to Get Control and Enjoy Life

You decided to start this journey and take a stand to get control over your eating, to stop living the life you were living and break out of the shell that had formed around you. Now, you are doing something about your issues and are making progress. Sometimes things take longer, and we all face speed bumps along the way, but with each step you take, you are getting closer to your goal weight.

Get excited about the fact that you are taking a stand!! You are taking the path less traveled and have joined the few that have decided to do what it takes to start living the life you want.

And, never forget, you have a wonderful life ahead of you and just by doing what you are doing, you are on your way!!!

Your Single Motivation

As you know, your journey will present you with a number of peaks and valleys in the way you are feeling. Your motivation will ebb and flow through the process of creating change. Try to get back to the core of your own personal motivation and never let go of that fire that got you started.

All or Nothing Personality

Do you consider yourself to have an all or nothing personality?

Let me explain....For me, the answer is resoundingly yes and it's the reason for not only my previous weight issues, but also many of the other issues in my life. While I definitely would not call myself an extremist, I do have a very strong tendency to overdo things.

As you can see, as I lost my weight, this was an incredibly important area of my life that needed to be addressed. Essentially, I had to ask myself why I had a tendency to go overboard with things. And, as you can guess, this same issue also impacted my life in many other areas. I really had to look at all of the behaviors in my life and come to an understanding of why I had to push everything to the limit. Of course, it's much easier said than done, but it's an important part of the transition process. And, for me, learning how to find the happy middle ground made an incredible difference in my life, weight loss success, and long-term maintenance.

Your diet is not just about losing the weight, but getting at the core issues of why you put it on to begin with. And, for many, the core issues are a direct result of how we decide to live our lives. Notice how I said the word, decide. Everything that we do is a decision. Sure, facing these issues is not easy, but if you decide to make the change, it can be done. For me, this was a decision that I had to come to terms with.

Create a More Balanced Life through Goals

I was sitting with my daughter reading her the "101 Dalmatians" and I couldn't help but think about how my life has changed from when I was my former heavy self. And, not from the perspective of having kids or anything that was new in my life, but more from the perspective of how balanced my life became. In my prior life as an all or nothing person, if I was ordering a steak or a piece of prime rib, I would always order the biggest cut on the menu. If something could be super sized, I would do it. At Christmas, not only did I cover the entire house with lights, but I also covered the lawn, trees, and everything else too. If we were having a BBQ, the bigger the fire the better. As you can see, balance was not something I had mastered in my life and my weight problem was a physical display of this issue.

As I lost weight, balance was an incredibly important area of my life that needed to be addressed. Essentially, I had to ask myself why did everything have to be all or nothing. While approaching the behaviors that were causing me to overeat and be overweight, I really had to look at all of the actions in my life.

With this knowledge about myself, I made a conscious effort to become what I like to call a balanced person. When I put my life in front of me, I made the decision that each part would be nurtured equally, and no part done in an overabundance. I set out to create a more balanced life, with the focus on goals in each of the following 5 areas:

- Family
- Work and Career
- Friends and Community
- Health and Fitness
- Me Time

Family: Family time was scheduled and put aside each day. So, no matter how hectic life became, the core foundation of our family would always be present; in our home that typically means between 5:30 - 7:30pm. I know it might not sound like a lot, but when it's consistent every night, it's something that I believe everyone can come to enjoy. In fact, it's allowed my wife and I to have some grounding, when things get out of hand in our careers.

Work and Career: Work time is Monday - Friday (and on the weekends too). But, no matter how crazy things are, it never gets in the way of family time. And, without a doubt, weekends are left for spending quality time together. Yes, I still work some very long hours, but I do it knowing that what I'm trading my time for has got to be important, as opposed to my previous thinking of working for the sake of working and achieving goals that would be forgotten about as quickly as they were achieved.

Friends and Community: Whether it's spending time with your friends, local community, or your church, this is an important part of life. Helping and being involved in the lives of others is very crucial to being a well rounded individual. Life is often very hard and without thinking about it, we can often find ourselves just looking out for "Numero-Uno". And, as anyone that is reading this knows, life sometimes has a way of becoming harder than any one person can handle. So, it's times like these where the investment in your friends and community is well worth the effort.

Health and Fitness: Just like any meeting that I have during the work day, going to the gym and getting in exercise has the same level of priority. In fact, for me, it's something that is scheduled like any meeting and I don't let anything get in the way of it. Yes, exceptions to the rule do exist, but for the most part, I take going to the gym each day as seriously as I take picking up my daughter from day care. It's just something that cannot be missed.

Me Time: While you may give 100% of yourself to everyone else in your life, it's critical for you to have some me time. Basically, the time of the day that is just for you. For me, I use my time at the gym as this time. Not only can I focus on my own health and fitness, but by making it "my time" in the day, it also allows me to enjoy it more. In fact, it's something that I just do for me. This time could just as easily be doing anything that you enjoy...Perhaps reading, knitting, or swimming. But regardless of the activity, it's important to have this time for you each day. And, in doing so, you'll find that the rest of your day spent working, supporting family, or helping others is that much easier because of the time that you have also invested in yourself.

Why Some People Succeed Where Others Fail...

Why do some people succeed where others fail? From my perspective, it all comes down to the person's mindset and their overall attitude.

While inspiration and motivation are great, they mean nothing without the right attitude. For many, they approach a diet from the feeling of being denied food. And, while this is correct, if people were to simply tweak this view a little bit, the outcome could be tremendous. Instead of seeing the diet as something that is denying you food, try viewing it as the opportunity of a lifetime. In fact, try to compare your opportunity to go on a diet like winning the lottery. You are in a very unique position, with resources at your disposal, to lose the weight and start living the life you have deserved for so long. This diet is not denying you food, it is taking you closer to the new you each day. The person who will look in the mirror and think how wonderful they look, will enjoy wearing clothes again, and will feel comfortable in everything they do.

This diet is giving you the opportunity to have that, and so much more. You have an amazing and very exciting life ahead of you and this diet will be just the first step in allowing you to enjoy all of it.

So, the next time you are around other people eating, don't feel bad...Feel proud!! Proud that you are taking on something that will give you back your self-confidence, and more importantly—give you a second chance on life.

While I realize this is unquestionably a mind shift from where many people are coming from, it's exactly the place you need to be to succeed. And the more you can put these thoughts into practice, the more exciting the diet will become and the more motivated you will be every day to do everything you can to be successful.

So, start getting excited and take back the life you want to be living!! And remember, success vs. failure is all about attitude.

Commitment, Not Weight Loss

I know this requires a little bit of mental shift, but I think it's important to look at your success from the perspective of how successful you are in sticking with a diet, and not with the weight loss.

For example, if you stick with your diet 100%, then you will be successful. And if you don't, then your weight loss will suffer. Of course, no matter how well you stick with the diet, some weeks will result in a lot of weight loss and other weeks it will slow down. So, my advice is this....

Simply forget about counting the pounds!!

For example, each week when you weigh-in, it should not concern you about how much you have lost. What matters most is that you stuck with the program 100%. And if the scale doesn't move as much as you like, simply know that your body was holding weight. Nine times out of ten, by just sticking with the program for another week, you'll find that the following week is more successful.

Therefore, while counting the number of pounds that you have lost is a great way to keep score, sometimes it can be depressing. In fact, since the weight never really comes off as fast as we would like, it's often easier to simply forget about it for a little while.

As you progress on your diet, try telling yourself the following:

"As long as I am doing everything in my power to be successful on the diet, I know the weight will come off."

For me, having faith in this one little statement is what made all the difference in the world.

Your Diet is No Big Deal!

To me, one of the biggest secrets to success was creating a mental attitude that regardless of how hard dieting was, I would never mentally acknowledge it. Sure, I might think about it, but on a day-to-day basis when I talked to people, I always took the position that it was no big deal.

It might seem very funny or odd, but the less emphasis I mentally placed on the diet, the easier the program was to stick with. For example, when anyone asked if the diet was hard, I would reply, "It's no big deal." Regardless of how hard the diet became, I would always reply "It's no big deal." It seemed that the more I repeated this message to people, the more I believed it myself.

In fact, I remember going out for dinner on a number of occasions and being surrounded by some of the most amazing foods. And I would simply suck on my shake with a smile. Of course, people would be in amazement that I could do this. But when they asked me how I could possibly stick with the diet around all the food, I would simply reply, "It's no big deal." While I was actually dying on the inside, taking this approach really gave me inner strength and conviction. I have no doubt that I was simply fooling myself and/or performing some sort of poor man's self-hypnosis, but after awhile, I actually believed that it was "no big deal."

Of course, as we all know, dieting is very challenging. But my point is that the more I took the position with others that it was "no big deal," the more I believed it myself. This approach became my self-fulfilling prophecy. The more I said it and lived it, the more it became a reality.

For me, going on this diet represented a final stand to win the battle against my weight and eating issues. This was my chance to fight the last fight and do whatever it was going to take. And to win, I realized that a key part of the process was to mentally condition myself to be strong and not to give in. To mentally say, "This diet is no big deal," no matter how hard it got. To never, never give up, until I reached my goal...and even then, continue to achieve success.

To do this, I tried to block out all self-defeating thoughts. Sure, I had hundreds of them, but I mentally battled through each one, continually repeating, "This diet is no big deal," or "If not now, when?" So, no matter how hard it got, I just continued to tell myself that it was "no big deal."

. . . .

Impacts of Our Motivations

We all understand and can relate to the burdens of being overweight. And, for most of us, we use these burdens to get started on our diets. Some examples include:

- Getting tired of how hard it is to shop for clothes.
- Getting tired of feeling self conscious when eating out.
- Getting tired of being socially or professionally invisible.
- Getting tired of putting your health at risk.
- Getting tired of being scared that you won't be around for a long time.
- Getting tired of not being able to play with your kids/grandkids.

These issues are what I would call internal factors that we deal with on a daily basis. Ultimately, many of these factors are what drove us to get started in losing the weight. However, another category exists. I like to call these factors the external factors. And these include:

- Getting started because of something someone said.
- Getting tired of the way people looked at us.
- Getting tired of the whispers.

- Getting started because of family harassment.
- Getting started because of jealousy or resentment.
- Getting started because of revenge.

The fact is, the world is full of people that are not very nice. And, as larger people, we have all experienced some degree of the way people can treat us from time to time. I've personally seen many people start their diets and successfully reach their goal weights because of these factors. These are huge personal motivators and nothing can be more powerful than:

- Wanting to show the person that has been harassing you that you could lose the weight and make them eat those words.
- Wanting to show them that you could lose the weight and be the one having the last laugh.
- Wanting to show the ex that they would be sorry for breaking up with you.
- Wanting to make the former friend feel sorry for the way they treated you.
- Wanting to make everyone at the reunion jealous and sorry that they weren't nice to you before.

And, while many of us may not have had the same degree of external factors that I listed above, the fact is that many of us got started on our diets because of our wives, husbands, friends, family, or whatever...Whether it was because of something someone said or something someone did, the fact is that someone probably helped push us into taking action.

The truth is that your long-term success will play greatly into the factors that drove you to your weight loss. Meaning, if the reasons that you got started were internally driven, then you'll have constant reminders around you as to the rewards of your hard work. However, if the reasons that drove you to your weight loss were externally driven, then the success and reward of your weight loss will be short lived.

So, regardless of the motivating factors that got you started, consider reshaping them into factors that will keep you motivated after reaching your goal weight.

. . . .

Consider How Lucky You Are

I have a good friend who is in the hospital and is suffering from a disease that is essentially killing him. Unfortunately, it's to the point that all he can really hope for now is to try and remain comfortable throughout the process. Anyway, each time that I see him, it reminds me of how lucky I am to have a problem that I can overcome. Allow me to explain...

Many people complain about the taste of diet products and this always makes me laugh a little. Sure, I'll be the first to say that having a good tasting product is essential, but it's also important to look at the products from a different perspective. Imagine having a disease that was killing you. One day you visit your doctor and he/she informs you that they have a cure. In fact, all you have to do is swallow 5-8 pills each day. The pills won't taste very good, but if you do this for a few months, you'll be cured of the disease. Would you complain? No, in fact, you would probably be jumping for joy! I know for my friend, he would give his left arm for this option.

Now, consider the consequences of your weight. Consider that over time if you don't take care of this problem it is going to kill you. However, you have an option!! All you have to do is follow your program. Sure, all programs may not have the best tasting products, but when you view them from this perspective, I can assure you that they'll taste great.

. . . .

Personal Ingredient 2: Staying In the Moment

As you learn to create your new lifestyle, it's important to begin the process of becoming self aware. Meaning, if you want to change, you must first have the ability to be conscious of your own actions, and more importantly, to evaluate and acknowledge your own success. So, as we discuss your second personal ingredient, we are examining the process of staying in the moment, which includes the following two components:

Being Aware of Yourself: This is the act of observing the behaviors that you want to change. Some examples of this might include eating late at night, snacking at work, or feeling like your eating is out of control. It can also be something that you aren't doing enough of, like exercising or drinking water. Regardless, the first step in overcoming these behaviors is to be aware of your actions and to practice staying in the moment when they occur. Whether we like it or not, bad habits can happen without us knowing it. So, by becoming self aware, you are in essence taking another step towards responsibility for all your actions.

Evaluate Yourself: The act of evaluating yourself is having the ability to review your ongoing actions against the goals that you want to achieve. This is an extremely important aspect since we cannot succeed at changing, unless we can first measure our success. By knowing your own goals, being self aware, and then evaluating yourself, you can continue to measure your progress.

With so many things that we do in life, we often get caught up in tempting situations. Then, before you know it, you have eaten something or behaved in a way that is contrary to the new lifestyle that you are trying to develop. So, the simple act of remaining in the moment is essential with everything that you do. Never forget the power of your second ingredient and with it, you can always ensure that you are conscious of your actions and conscious of how you are reacting to situations.

Chapter Three

Getting Into the Right Mindset

"I have not failed. I've just found 10,000 ways that won't work."

— Thomas Alva Edison

One of the biggest mistakes that people make when dieting is to overly focus on their weight loss and the importance of what the scale is showing. Yes, we are all in this game to lose weight, but your focus cannot just be on the scale or true success will always be out of your grasp. For example, each of us has either lost weight and gained it back, or knows someone that has also done this. Clearly, while going through the process of losing weight is never easy, if someone has the right mindset and discipline, they can be successful. However, just losing the weight is clearly not enough and this is where most people go wrong. Instead of viewing your time on a diet as just a time to lose weight, consider it a time that you do some true reflection and determine the reasons behind your weight issues, and more importantly, the new behaviors and goals that you want to accomplish for yourself.

For some, it's simply a matter of eating less and adding exercise back into their life. And, for others, their diet provides a unique experience to take a step away from food and approach the relationship from a new and healthier perspective. Regardless, what matters the most is to make the journey and behavioral changes a point of reflection when you have reached your goal weight.

The bottom line is this; you have the power to lose your weight, and to also keep it off for the rest of your life. But it's going to require breaking the mold. It's going to require reflection and honesty towards your own issues and getting to the root of what has caused you to be overweight. And, while it's never fun to look inward and examine our own vulnerabilities and issues, doing this is going to allow you to achieve success.

. . . .

Viewing Food Differently

I want to present you with a challenge to start looking at food differently. When I look back on my own personal life cycle and views of food, my mindset changed in the following order:

Start: Very excited about what I was doing for myself, but missed my old comfort foods and was not happy about it. In fact, it often made me very annoyed.

Beginning Phase: Still longed for my old comfort foods and couldn't really see myself happy in life without them.

Midway Point: Began to realize that I was perfectly fine without the foods that I used to turn to for support, comfort, or when stressed.

Last Mile: Came to the realization that I could enjoy anything I wanted, but I just needed to enjoy things in moderation and have checks and balances in my life.

Goal Weight: Came to the understanding that if I enjoyed a treat, it had consequences. Meaning, if I wanted a moment of bliss, it meant 30 minutes on the treadmill. And nothing is worth that!

Maintenance and Transition (year 1): Had insight that the foods that I put into my body have a direct impact on my overall body composition. The more I ensured I was eating lean meats, vegetables, and working out consistently, the more progress I made at the gym and the better I looked.

Maintenance and Transition (year 2-4): Came to such an appreciation of how nutrition can impact your body that I have truly become grossed out by many of the things that I once loved. In fact, while I certainly do still enjoy the occasional treat, some foods are simply nasty and I refuse to touch them. Of course, the majority of these foods that I feel this way about are the same foods that I used to snuggle up with for temporary comfort or stress management.

Maintenance and Transition (the rest of your life): Came to the understanding that life is always going to present situations that are difficult and that I'll always have a natural inclination to want to comfort myself with food. However, these feelings are certainly not as strong as when I started, and although they may never go away, it does not mean that I have to give in to them. In fact, in looking forward, I have simply come to recognize them as part of who I am and a part of my personality that makes me unique. But what matters most is never turning your back on these feelings and simply having the ability to acknowledge them and learn to manage them. Basically, in front of me now is a life of healthy eating, exercise, and having fun. And what could be better then that?

My point with this walk down memory lane is to hopefully demonstrate the changes in my own thought processes over the years. What made the biggest difference for me was changing my views on food. When I no longer viewed food and nutrition from the perspective of just weight loss, I achieved an understanding of how food and nutrition could help me to change the look of my body.

As you progress, don't think for a moment that you have to wait until you have reached your goal weight to begin this new mindset. In fact, I only wish that I had started down the path sooner. So, with each healthy meal you enjoy, think about the food, what it is doing for you and how you can take advantage of it through exercise and fitness. The more you see the results in the mirror, the more you'll see the results in the way you are thinking and reacting in a different manner to the foods that you once loved.

. . . .

Create an Image of Yourself

Close your eyes after reading this and create a mental picture of yourself at your goal weight. And, as much as possible, try and focus on the clothes that you are wearing and the activity you are doing. In fact, just think about the words "goal weight" and allow the image to come into focus.

Alright...this should only take 3-5 seconds. Now, hold onto this image! No, it's not something you can frame or put on your desk. But when you need a brief reminder of what you are working for, know that you can recreate this image at anytime. And, more importantly, never forget the importance of this image. In fact, like anything in life, if you can imagine it, you can create it.

. . . .

Think in Terms of Commitment, Not Pounds

Let's face it, nothing is more fun than seeing the progress of your hard work on the scale each week. When it comes to long-term success and giving yourself the ability to look through plateau points, it's important to view your success from the perspective of sticking with the diet as opposed to the weight loss.

If you stick with your diet 100%, then you will be successful. And if you don't, then your weight loss will suffer. Of course, no matter how well you stick with the diet, some weeks will result in a big weight loss and other weeks will result in a small weight loss. So, my advice is this....

Forget about the scale and focus on the journey.

Each week when you weigh-in, don't concern yourself with how much you have lost. What matters most is that you stuck with the program 100%. And if the scale doesn't move as much as you like, know that your body is holding weight. By just sticking with the program for another week, you'll find that the following week is that much more successful.

As you progress on your diet, try telling yourself the following:

"As long as I am doing everything in my power to be successful on the diet, I know the weight will come off."

For me, having faith in this one statement is what made all the difference in the world.

Hitting Rock Bottom

The realization that a problem exists often comes at the most unusual times. For some, it comes when they look in a mirror, or see a picture of themselves, but for me, it came on a weekend trip to Las Vegas.

On this particular trip, my wife and I decided, as a joke, to go and have what Las Vegas refers to as the world's largest hot dog. It's about 2 feet long, fully loaded, and totally insane. I eventually got my hot dog, and decided that nothing washes down a hot dog better than a 20 oz Pina Colada. With provisions in hand, I sat down with my wife at a slot machine, and proceeded to light up a cigar. If it sounds like I was out of control, I was.

For about 20 minutes I sat at the slot machine chomping my 2 foot hotdog, drinking my Pina Colada, and smoking my cigar. Not surprisingly, I started to sweat and feel poorly. It seems that through all my slot machine playing, pork byproduct eating, and coconut/rum drinking, I had worked myself into exhaustion. In only 20 minutes, I was a mere shell (same size shell, just not the same pizzazz) of my former self.

Sitting there, I felt very tired, very hot, and very weak. In fact, my wife looked over at me and said that I was the spitting image of Elvis.

"During the good years?" I asked.

Unfortunately, her reply was not something I wanted to hear: "No, right before he went to the bathroom upstairs at his house."

It was at that moment, the moment I was compared to Elvis that I knew I had hit rock bottom. Most importantly, it was time to find a solution. And the rest is history.

. . . .

Climbing Mt. Everest

I was listening to the radio and I heard a great statement from a rock climber about the discipline and mental attitude that was required to climb Mount Everest. In listening to him, I noticed some similarities between his story and what many of us face as we begin the journey of tackling our weight issues.

The one thing that he said that was right on target for me was his thoughts on the attitudes of the mountain climbers. In essence, he felt that the people who started the climb with the internal belief that they would be happy if they only made it half way up the mountain typically only made it to the half way point, turned around and came back down the mountain. However, the people who started the journey and kept their sights on reaching the peak typically didn't stop until they reached the top. Attitude was the main difference between the two groups.

I often hear people say that they would be happy losing half of their goal weight instead of all of it. It's very interesting when you think about it. Sometimes I have set my goals lower than what I thought I could accomplish. I'm not sure why I've done this in the past, but I imagine it's a self preservation mechanism against failure. Regardless, this diet is not one of those times...This is the time to look to the top of the mountain and set your sights on reaching it!!

From this day forward make the top of the mountain your goal and don't let anything stop you from reaching it. Remember, you only have one life to live, and now is the time to start living it. Just think of the view from the top of the mountain. You'll have your entire life ahead of you and you'll be able to take the new you and go on and pursue other dreams and goals and start living life to its fullest.

What's Stopping You?

When I started my diet, I had 100 pounds to lose and because the journey seemed so overwhelming, I completely removed the thought of my end goal from my mind and only focused on the week to week progress.

When I started, I tried not to set predetermined objectives, but to just stay focused on one thing: STAY ON THE DIET NO MATTER WHAT.

I knew that if I did this, it was physically impossible for my body not to lose weight. As luck would have it, the weight came off quickly, but I never expected it and ONLY stayed focused on sticking with the program. In fact, whenever I found the diet hard, I would say the following thing....

"If I don't succeed this time, when will I be successful?"

I know this is an all or nothing approach, but I felt that this was the approach that I needed to take to be successful. I had no excuse not to succeed and ultimately the only person who could stop me from being successful was me.

This is the attitude that I think it takes to be successful. Don't treat your diet as another attempt at losing the weight; treat it as an exciting experience that is going to change your life. No matter how hard it gets, nothing can stop you from your goal. Take on a new attitude toward your diet today, and keep it going!!

. . . .

Make A Personal Vow!

We all approach our diets from different backgrounds and perspectives. I believe everyone needs the right mindset and overall attitude to be successful. I consider this to be the single biggest difference between those that reach their goal and those that do not.

If you have been feeling discouraged and feeling like the road ahead is a long one, try viewing your diet from a new perspective. View it as the opportunity of a lifetime.

Next time you chew on a celery stick while others are eating pizza, don't feel bad...Feel proud!! Proud that you are taking on something that will give you back your self-confidence.

For me, whenever I felt down or felt like the road ahead was too long to manage, I would remind myself of the following...Now is the time to take a stand and start changing my life, and each moment that I stay true to the diet is a step closer to my new life.

I think it's time that you consider making a personal vow to yourself. Don't worry, no one will see you doing this, but by making a personal vow, you will strengthen your commitment. Whether you are at work, at home, sitting in traffic, sitting on the couch, or in bed...Take a moment and make the following vow to yourself:

"Today, I'm making a personal promise that nothing is going to stop me from reaching my goal weight and being successful on this diet. I understand that this is going to take sacrifice on my part, and on the part of my family, but now is the time to take back my life. I've waited long enough and have put my life on hold for far too long. I'm making this personal vow for myself to myself."

See Yourself as a Diet Athlete

The challenge of being successful on any program is finding the individual motivation that drives you. What might be motivating for one person is often not motivating for someone else.

I approached the diet as a sort of final mission at a mid-way point in my life to test myself. To see if I really had what it takes to cross a hurdle accomplished by few. While I didn't know where the journey would take me, I had faith that if I could survive this and come out the other side successfully, the rewards would go far beyond weight loss.

The rest is history and I'm glad to say that I went the distance and lost the weight. I set a goal for myself and accomplished it. The feeling of reaching my goal weight with all the hardship and sacrifice goes down in my book as one of the greatest accomplishments of my life, better than championship games, college graduation, professional accomplishments, and a list of other proud moments. Reaching my goal weight was a life changing experience. It changed the way I looked and felt, and it changed my outlook on life. I felt that I could accomplish anything.

Dieting Is Like Playing Poker

If you can view your weight loss as secondary to staying on the program, things will be easier!

For example, by focusing on the program instead of the weight loss, it's easier to achieve a long-term view and become comfortable in the process. And the best part, the more you focus on the program, the more your body will take care of dropping the weight. Since we ultimately don't control this process, or at least how our bodies respond, the one thing we can control is how successful we are at sticking to the program.

To make my point, the following is a real world example of this...I play poker on a fairly regular basis. When I play, I strive to play perfect cards. My goal is not how much money I take out of the game, but how perfect my game is. What is really funny about this is that if I focus on my game play and not on the money, the money will always follow. And, in terms of dieting, by focusing on the program and not on the day-to-day weight loss, your personal weight loss will follow.

Do It for Yourself

I had the pleasure of watching my friend Robb go through the process of trying to stop smoking. And although I had never considered the similarities between the process of someone trying to stop smoking and someone getting control over their eating, it was an interesting process to witness. Like myself and the process of trying to lose weight and gain control, Robb had also tried to quit smoking many times in the past and was not successful. However, just like myself, Robb ultimately had a light bulb moment in that he decided to not quit smoking for anyone else but himself. In the past, we had both been unsuccessful in that we were trying to do something very difficult to please others. And whenever you try to do something as hard as gaining control over your own cravings and creating new behaviors, you have to be doing it for yourself. In fact, you are the only one that will ever be able to give yourself the true motivation and strength to carry forward. But in making the decision to overcome something on your own with the desire to do it for yourself, you are ultimately taking back control. No longer can anyone influence your feelings on the subject or give you an excuse or permission to fail. In taking on the objective yourself, you are giving yourself the power to be successful regardless of what situations you face or the feelings or actions of others around you.

When overcoming anything, it's extremely easy to allow the feelings of our family and friends to influence us. And when it comes to weight loss, your success can often bring out jealousy and desires to sabotage what you have accomplished. Unfortunately, in being successful, you can become a physical reminder to others around you as to what they should already be doing for themselves. And, as a result, they will often try to cause you to fail to avoid having to face the same issues. So, in taking back control and setting your goals for yourself, you are taking back the power and allowing yourself to be successful no matter how much or how little support you might have.

Timing

Most of us, before starting a diet, spend a great deal of time thinking about the diet, trying to create the perfect circumstance for starting. For most, this means finding the best time when life won't be too hectic, and you'll have the proper focus to be successful. Let's face it, no one wants to fail. And since most people have been on previous diets, they are all too aware of the commitment and dedication that it takes to succeed.

Unfortunately, what tends to happen while we are waiting for this perfect moment is that time begins to pass. Yes, we have all the best intentions and reasons for waiting, but we usually don't start because we don't want to let ourselves down. We want to be successful and in our fear of failure, we end up sitting on the sidelines and waiting instead of starting the diet. We know that we have made the decision to go on a diet, so then we actually begin to eat more, as if telling ourselves that since we will be starting a diet soon, it's alright to enjoy a little bit extra right now. Our best intentions become a very vicious cycle. For some, this cycle of deciding to go on a diet, but never truly starting, can lead to years of good intentions and continued weight gain.

Starting the diet is one of the most liberating things that you will ever do for yourself. Just by taking baby steps, one foot in front of the other, you can look at yourself in the mirror and know that you are doing everything in your power to be successful, and that whether you are ready or not, you are doing it!!! Think in terms of the Nike slogan..."Just do it!" Yes, taking the first step may seem scary, but the truth of the matter is that after you have done it, you'll realize it wasn't so bad. Then, you'll have made it through the first day, then, a few days, then, a week! And, having accomplished that, you'll come to the realization that you are losing weight and taking back control of your life. With this knowledge comes power...You have the power to be successful.

The Secret to Getting Started

As anyone knows, the most difficult part of dieting is starting. So, I wanted to take a few moments and talk about this. First off, very few people deciding to go on a diet start and don't stop until they reach their goal weight. The fact is, most people actually start the process a few years earlier and try dipping their toes in the water.

I know for myself, I followed a very ugly cycle of starting and stopping diets over and over again. In fact, I can remember many Sunday nights telling myself, "The diet starts tomorrow," only to have a successful start and find that by noon I was already off the wagon. Of course, since I had slipped, I then had the rest of the week to prepare for the next Monday attempt again. In fact, if I had a dime for every time I tried that scenario, I would have a truck full of change. Personally, I found that the cycle of this exercise was extremely ugly and also very hard to break. As many of you know, I was able to do it. But it took hard work and discipline. However, if you want to get started and not stop, here is the formula for success:

First, I decided to treat each day of the diet as its own day. I wouldn't look to the next day, but treat each moment as the here and now. I personally believed that if I could make it through the next ten minutes, two hours, or next meal, then I could continue on. While I spent many moments looking at my shakes and comparing them to the rest of the food in the fridge, I ultimately took the path of the shakes, if only to prove to myself that I could overcome the temptation and continue forward. Yes, this was a constant battle, but the more time I put into the program without falling off the wagon, the easier it got. In fact, after a few weeks of being successful, the fear of falling off the wagon and resorting back to old habits was enough to keep me honest. Personally, even a month into the program, I knew that if I cheated, I would probably head into a downward spiral that would definitely include our neighborhood all-you-can-eat Chinese buffet. And, since I was honest enough to know my own weaknesses, I found it easier not to tempt those demons. It's amazing how one can be doing so well on a diet and achieving a level of mental satisfaction, only to be derailed by a simple tootsie roll or three cent mint. Anyway, in a nutshell, it all comes down to focusing on the moment, not looking ahead, but simply being aware of your present situation and staying focused to ensure that you stick with the diet.

Now, the good news is that once you've started your diet and are doing it on a regular basis the changes in your body will be the ultimate motivation for keeping you on track. In fact, you'll feel so good about yourself that you'll defend your new habits at all costs and have the motivation to continue. You'll soon be looking back, having lost 50, 70, and 100 pounds and wondering where the time went. And you'll have done it all by simply keeping your head down and staying focused on the moment!

. . . .

When Things Get Hard

When things get hard and you feel temptation knocking at the door, take a moment and make the following promise to yourself:

"I promise that I have started my diet to change my life. I'm 100% committed to this and I'm doing it for me. I want to change my life and I understand that it's going to take sacrifice and hard work, but I'm worth it. This is the place in time that I've chosen to do this. Not tomorrow, or next week, but right now."

Never forget that before you is the opportunity to make up for past starts and stops. No more excuses!! Bottom line, now is the time to seize the moment and make your diet the start of a very new and exciting life.

Personal Ingredient 3: Talk to Yourself

As you are now learning, the secret to being successful with your new lifestyle is to develop new behaviors that last. Unfortunately, creating new behaviors is not an easy process. But it can be done! Of course, in order to create new behaviors, it is extremely important to create reminders that will ensure your success. Let's face it, we get used to certain behaviors and it's extremely difficult to break loose and create new ones. So, by creating reminders, we can constantly prompt ourselves to recall our new goals and allow ourselves to be successful.

While we surround ourselves with all sorts of physical reminders in our lives, the most powerful ones are the things that we say to ourselves. Within each of us are the words that are strong enough to enable us to do anything. Of course, the secret is to be able to unlock your own words and find the ones that work for you. A few examples include:

"I'm going to stick with this diet and reach my goal weight."

"Now is the time!"

"Nothing tastes as good as thin feels."

"If I don't change my life now, when will I?"

Think about the things that mean the most to you and create a set of your own personal reminders. Perhaps pictures of your kids or family provide motivation, or pictures of you at your goal weight, or current weight. For some, these types of reminders are very powerful in creating daily motivation. Next, come up with your own personal words to help yourself when faced with challenging situations. Remember, when it's 2:00 a.m. and nothing stands between you and a carton of ice cream, having something that you say to yourself can have a very powerful impact in getting past the situation. Amazingly, when you begin to implement these reminders and successfully overcome the challenges in your life, you'll soon realize that nothing can stop you. You'll achieve a new sense of empowerment and an understanding that you are truly going to reach your goal weight and develop a new lifestyle that you can enjoy for the rest of your life. Having the ability to talk to yourself and learning how to use this ingredient at key moments in your life is often the difference between sticking to your plan and new lifestyle and taking another step backwards. So, as you move forward and further develop your own personal dialogue, never forget that the encouragement that you provide yourself is often the most powerful.

Chapter Four

Taking Responsibility

"The great thought, the great concern, the great anxiety of men is to restrict, as much as possible, the limits of their own responsibility."

— Giosue

Try to put a label on what food means to you. You know the food you turn to when trying to cope with life situations. Typically, this isn't the food that you eat for meals, but the in-between or snack food that you eat when you are alone. For myself, I used food as a moment of escape. When things got stressful in my life (whether at work or home), I would quickly find myself with a muffin, ice cream, or crackers in hand. I would turn to food as a form of resentment. If something annoyed me, instead of dealing with the issue, I would put something into my mouth. And, last but not least, I also used food as a form of rebellion. If someone commented on my weight or said something rude, I would eat to show them who was boss.

I used food to deal with all sorts of issues in my life. To me, eating was a physical escape. It was a moment of bliss that I could enjoy and that I thought would make me feel better. Snacks were a kind of mini drug for me.

As I dealt with these issues, I came to an understanding of what was going on, but until I figured out what snacking meant to me, it was hard to control my situation and begin to make progress.

I found that as soon as I was able to verbalize what the muffins, crackers, or other goofy foods represented, I could view them in a different light. So, if I found myself turning to those snacks to cope with any situation, I was instantly able to view them as my drug. And for me...this changed everything!

Viewing Other Heavy People

One of the strangest things that I have found about losing weight is the way I look at heavy people now. When I was 100 pounds overweight, I typically looked at heavy people as if they were lazy or had no self control, but I was their same size; I just didn't see myself. In fact, it wasn't until I took off the weight that I was able to reflect and admit how large I really was. I certainly wasn't lazy or lacking in self discipline, I just had extremely bad eating habits and a love for large portions. Now when I see a person who is equal to my old size, I definitely look at them with a feeling of connection. I can relate closely to how they are feeling and how the world is treating them. Don't get me wrong, I'm no diet evangelist, just someone who is concerned for others and wishes that everyone could experience the feeling of control that I possess now.

The Monday Syndrome

One of the most frequent comments I hear during the spring is that people want to start a diet to get ready for the summer. While this sounds admirable, one of the concerns I always have is if you don't start your diet until summer, you won't reach your goal weight until the end of summer. One of the unfortunate fall-outs of this is what I would call the "Monday" syndrome. I'll start my diet this Monday...or, I'll start my diet at the end of the month... or, I'll start the diet during the fall. I was probably the worst offender of this Monday Syndrome, always coming up with excuses for waiting until whenever to start the diet. The Monday Syndrome is a slippery slope and should be dealt with post haste.

The Importance of Accountability

The amazing thing about accountability when going through the process of losing weight and gaining control in your life is that we can often be our own best friends and worst enemies at the same time. Meaning, each of us personally holds the power to be successful in anything that we do; however, we also hold the power to provide ourselves with excuses and make promises that we know we won't keep. Think about it, how many times have you eaten something and promised yourself that you would go to the gym or workout the next day? Or, promised yourself that you would lose weight and stick to your diet, but only find yourself putting off starting the process or not holding yourself accountable? Some people have the strength and determination to be self disciplined; however, for the rest of us, having some accountability in our life can make all the difference between failure and success.

So, in order to be successful with your own progress, it's important to do the very painful act of asking someone for help and accountability. For many people, this is the very reason that they go to weight loss clinics. They don't necessarily need to pay the high cost of the products, but what they are truly seeking is the accountability of knowing that someone is waiting to see them each week and will be monitoring their progress. Yes, this sort of service costs a premium, but for some, it's often easier to lose the weight for fear of letting someone else down, rather then themselves. In fact, this was one of the underlying reasons that I started the free discussion board that can be accessed via the New Lifestyle Diet site—for the simple purpose of providing people with a place to go and feel supported and understood. A place to share one's daily, weekly, or monthly success, track their weight loss, and provide the same level of accountability and understanding to others. For some, sharing one's feelings in a group setting within a clinic is fantastic and will work wonders. But for others that don't have the time or money for such services, being able to have accountability online can make all the difference in their success. Of course, accountability can also be found through those around you…your neighbors, your husband/wife, or friends. Whomever you choose, it should be someone that you can report to on a regular basis who will always be available to you and will not be judgmental.

Definitely don't underestimate the power of accountability in your own life and take the time to determine who or what resources around you will allow you to be successful and stay on track.

Keep a Picture of Yourself

On the refrigerator in our kitchen, I keep one of my "big" pictures on the door with a magnet. When I started the diet, I saw it as a bitter reminder of why I was living my life through a straw. It definitely was not a picture that I was proud of, but an effective reminder of what I was trying to escape from. Of course, I always considered it just a bad picture, and not a true representation of what I looked like (yeah, right).

For months this agonizing picture sat on the fridge, seemingly haunting me on a daily basis. And, over time, it actually became sort of funny. While I was losing the weight, new friends would view it in disbelief and my wife would never miss the opportunity to show it to me if I looked like I was going to enter the kitchen for mischief. Now the source of shame and bitter reminder of my larger state of affairs has become a source of pride.

The picture will forever sit on the fridge and will probably always remain a silent reminder in case I ever forget.

. . . .

Taking Responsibility

I believe that each of us must take personal responsibility for our weight issues and for the discipline that is required for losing the weight. Trust me on this, if you are anything like me, you have probably asked yourself a thousand times why you are overweight. For me, I think I originally came up with every answer in the book including:

- My parents are overweight, so it's in the genes.
- I was an overweight kid; so obviously, I would be an overweight adult.
- I've been on so many diets that I caused damage to my metabolism.
- Diets don't work for me.

It's very easy to look around and come up with an excuse as to why you are or were overweight. What matters most is that you get to the bottom of your problem. Ultimately, I came to the realization that the buck stops here. I ate to comfort myself, I ate to handle stress, and I didn't exercise enough. And when you add all those factors together, it equals being overweight. When I placed blame where it belonged, and took personal responsibility, I was able to lose the weight, and keep it off and change my life forever.

. . . .

Say Good-bye to Food as a Friend

Food can often become a friend in our lives that is always available. It always listens, it never fights back, and although the conversations are one sided, the feeling of knowing that you have that friend always available can be very enticing. But, besides the obvious issues of gaining weight, one of the bigger issues of having food as a friend is that it can often become a barrier to other social avenues in our lives and even cause us to shelter ourselves from the world. Meaning, if you are someone who has treated food in your life like a friend, it's very easy to ignore other relationships and continue to turn to this source of comfort instead of growing as an individual with other people and experiences in your life.

Of course, breaking this chain is easier said than done. But, like any bad relationship, it's often important to step away from the situation and re-approach the relationship again with a new mindset. So, as you progress on your diet, you may find it hard at first to break the ties with some of your favorite comfort foods/friends, but it's critical to do this. It's important to begin to live again and not shelter yourself from the true joys in life that can only come from family, friends, and the little accomplishments that you create for yourself along the way. And while food may taste good and provide a moment of comfort, it will never replace the joys in life that you will find in other places. Now, this is not to say that food should not be celebrated or enjoyed. It should, but done with a new appreciation of what it does and does not bring to your life.

Personal Ingredient 4: Emotions and Cravings

For most dieters, learning how to control food cravings as they relate to their emotions is very difficult. The cravings are often brought on by television commercials or by driving past a certain restaurant. Cravings are a very real thing and if not controlled can often lead to a feeling of being out of control. So, if you are sitting here reading this and feeling in agreement—don't worry!!! Nothing is wrong with you, and with your fourth personal ingredient you'll soon be on your way to being back in control.

As you can imagine, when stressful situations occur, we often feel an immediate desire to eat. Of course, we'll often convince ourselves that we are hungry, when in actuality, we are simply comforting ourselves with food to get past a stressful moment in our lives. Unfortunately, in doing this, we teach ourselves that if eating can provide comfort in our lives for the bigger stresses, it can certainly also work for the little things. Then, before you know it, you are using food to handle just about everything. Whether it's a visit to the office vending machine, passing through your local drive through, or the extra muffin when buying coffee, it's very easy to begin comforting yourself throughout the day. Then, before you know it, you not only have a weight problem, but also the added burden of having to learn how to deal with stressful situations again without the comfort of food by your side. Obviously, food is not a federally regulated drug; however, when you look at the way that it is often used by individuals for comfort, you can quickly see how it can be addictive.

Adding to your personal ingredients list, keep a running tally of all of your cravings and the emotions or events behind them. The purpose of this is to allow you to begin recognizing the difference between real and emotional hunger.

So, how is this done????

Start being aware of what is going on around you; the more you can isolate your cravings and begin to dissect them, the more you'll be able to get control of the behavior. When you find yourself faced with a craving, ask the following two critical questions:

- What is my mood?
- Am I really hungry?

As you can see, the questions are not difficult. However, the real challenge is to learn how to be aware of what is happening to you and to have the ability to ask yourself these questions when they matter the most. Obviously, this is easier said than done, but the more you put these questions to use, the more you'll be in the drivers seat. Remember, creating a new lifestyle filled with new behaviors is not something that is developed overnight. It requires practice and commitment and begins by making a promise that you will be honest and will ask hard questions on a daily basis. And, in doing so, you'll find that you are soon approaching your cravings from an entirely new perspective and discovering a new sense of self awareness and understanding.

Chapter Five

Overcoming Temptation

"Tis one thing to be tempted and another thing to fall."
— William Shakespeare

As we travel on our own personal journey, each of us will face many moments of discovery. To me, no moment seems as important as what I like to call the Aha moment. You know, that moment a situation or event occurs when you realize you can do this! The moment that you realize you are going to be successful and that nothing can stop you. This moment can be one of the most memorable as you start your diet.

My Aha moment came when I was dieting and my wife asked me to take a couple dozen chocolate chip cookies into the office to share with everyone. Of course, I usually would have eaten half of them during the drive to the office, but I was so focused on my own personal mission, that I didn't even give the cookies a second thought. In fact, the Aha moment didn't even hit me until later in the day when my wife called and asked me how many of the cookies made it. To which I proudly replied, "All of them!"

Tempting Situations

Each morning in my former life, I would stop at a store on my way to work and start the day off with a cup of coffee and a donut, and then on the way home, I would stop at the same store and buy a Twix and another cup of coffee. As you know, a man needs to keep nourished for the long drive home. I felt content driving to or from work—especially knowing that the little store was never too far away. Yes...it's a very sad caffeine and sugar story.

When I made the decision to change my life and I started the process of losing the weight, I discovered a unique challenge that proved to be very difficult to overcome. Whenever I got close to the store that used to be my snack stop, my mind returned to those temptations. For some reason, just seeing the store or getting into that neighborhood caused a sort of Pavlov's dog reaction. My mouth would water and I'd get all excited.

Time eventually eased this problem for me. But it took a considerable amount of time before I was living my life in a different way, and those old urges and feelings went away.

And, to add insult to injury, around this same time, my wife got a car with a GPS system. The GPS would either announce or show a display map of every restaurant that the car was either approaching or passing. So we took my car until I was able to figure out how to disable this fun little feature.

To be successful on any diet, you must first learn to overcome your own thoughts and urges. For me, this has been one of my hardest challenges.

When dieting, it's important to remember that we are actually learning how to reprogram ourselves. We are learning that it's not alright to eat whatever we want and that we actually must show some restraint. In fact, not just some, but a lot of restraint!! I often find myself in the kitchen or out and about and my mind will start wandering about crackers or a little something. It all seems so innocent, but it's not. To be successful on a diet, you must have the ability to say NO!!!!

To say, "I know that I want to eat that cracker, but I'm not going to. I'm going to stick with this diet!!"

I know that when I started the process of losing weight, I found myself saying this little phrase about 10 times a day. Of course, I replaced the word cracker with countless other items (cookies, doughnuts, chips, beer, chicken wings, Taco Bell, etc.), but the message was still the same. And, as I progressed on the diet, things did get easier. Even today, I still find myself occasionally talking to myself. Which of course, I now view as a badge of honor!

A Challenge for Success

I had the unique experience of talking to a woman who was having a very hard time following her diet. And, as much as she tried, she continuously found herself eating things that were hurting her success. She seemingly could not find the strength to stop herself. And, in doing so, she had become incredibly discouraged and upset. While on the phone, I convinced her to get on her scale and check her weight. Not surprisingly, she discovered that even though she had not followed the program 100%, she had still lost weight. As you can imagine, she was overjoyed and felt a renewed sense of accomplishment.

Now, on the surface, this story would appear to have a happy ending. However, if you look closer, you'll discover that while this person had continued to lose weight, they made no progress in overcoming their real eating issues.

It is extremely common for people to be disciplined with their diets, and still allow themselves to give in to temptations.

I challenge you to **STOP**! When you find yourself giving in to temptations, **STOP**! Then point yourself back in the right direction.

Flexing Your Temptation Muscle

As everyone knows, the hardest part of starting a weight loss program, or being successful on one, is having the ability to stop yourself from giving in to temptation. For many, this single factor is often the reason for failure.

The first thing to remember is that like any muscle that hasn't been used for a while, self control can only get stronger with use. Therefore, instead of seeing temptation as the evil trap that can derail you, see it as a part of your new workout. Each time that you are faced with a temptation, see it as a mini-gym workout for your self-control. While this may seem odd...the truth is that the more you flex this muscle, the easier the exercise becomes.

Amazingly, by just being in the moment with your temptations and having the ability to STOP and not give in to them, you will discover an amazing thing....Nothing bad happened!!! The birds keep chirping, the earth keeps spinning, and that item that seemed so tempting at the time really does nothing for your overall happiness. In fact, you'll soon discover that nothing tastes better than lean and healthy! And as you face off temptation another amazing thing will happen to you....You'll find that you enjoyed the process.

Keep a List of Temptations

I was going over my notes from my diet and I came across my wish list. Whenever temptation came my way, I would add it to my ongoing wish list. I tried to avoid such situations, but often it was me against the apple pie. Worthy adversaries, but ones that I could not give in to, so I wrote down the food that I wanted to eat, with the hope of one day having it again. In doing this, I found two things. For each thing I wrote on my list, it represented an opportunity of temptation that I was able to overcome. Secondly, I seemed to find something very rewarding in writing down the food that was tempting me.

Now, as I look back and review my list, the items all sound fairly silly, and surprisingly, the majority of them I would never even consider eating now. Having the list helped me through some hard times and ultimately proved to be a ledger for how far I had come. I definitely would recommend this to everyone.

Cheating After Your Weekly Weigh-In

One of the most difficult things for me to stop was the temptation to cheat after my weekly weigh-in. Previously on other programs, I would follow the rules religiously all week until the weigh-in. Then, after the weekly weigh-in, I would go out to dinner with my wife. I was able to justify this by thinking I had lost another week's worth of weight and would have another week to burn off whatever I ate that night. In fact, this weekly cheat program went on for the majority of the time I followed other programs. On my final diet, I decided early on that I would follow the program 100%. The urges were still there, but I didn't repeat this cycle, even though the temptation was always present.

Creating a No-No Cabinet

After I started my diet, we decided that it would be best for everyone in the house if we locked up the crackers, cookies, candy, and all of the rest of the good stuff in a special cabinet. To do this, we took a few plastic safety straps and locked the cabinet. After doing this, we then referred to the cabinet as the "no-no cabinet."

So, after putting the straps on the cabinet, the only way to get in was to cut the straps. And since my wife took the straps into her office, I was basically out of luck. Also, to prevent me from going down to Home Depot and buying my own replacement straps, she also got special colored ones. Yep, that's what I call support; or she was just tired of me eating her cookies. Either way, the "no-no cabinet" was well secured.

We kept the straps on the cabinet for more time than I care to remember and finally decided that it was time to remove them. So, in cutting the straps, you can imagine my surprise to see the amount of stuff my wife had been hiding. Opening the cabinet was like hitting Willie Wonka's secret stash. It seems that every time my wife bought cookies or candy from any of the neighborhood kids, she immediately put it into the "no-no cabinet." Add that with all the other stuff she brought into the house and we basically had enough goodies in the cabinet to run our own movie concession stand.

When we opened the cabinet, I think my wife sensed the immediate tension in the air. While I thought I had a fairly good poker face, I must have come off like some sort of shark smelling blood in the water. Instead of a wounded fish, I was circling the kitchen, with intent to do harm on countless boxes of unsupervised Girl Scout cookies. Needless to say, I decided to escape down to Starbucks for a large black coffee.

Upon my return, I discovered that while my wife had not put the safety straps back on the "no-no cabinet," she did do the next best thing. She used our Food Saver Plus (big shrink wrapping machine) to shrink wrap everything. It seems that while I had no problem breaking into boxes of cookies or crackers in the house, I would not go out of my way to ruin my dieting progress. So, the extra shrink wrap kept me in check.

I saw the removal of the safety straps as a step in the right direction. Of course, working through step two—not having to shrink wrap the goodies—took a little longer to overcome. But I'm very pleased to report that the goodies are now openly available.

You Know you're Cheating When...

I want to remind you that cheaters never win. Trust me, I've seen or heard it all when it comes to diet cheating. So, in the spirit of my own years of cheating, the following is a very small list of cheating moments that you may or may not even be aware of:

- You're testing your family's food while cooking it.
- You're testing the batter while baking.
- You're having a spoonful of peanut butter, because you "need the protein."
- You're eating the tops off of the chocolates, but not the insides. It doesn't count if you don't eat the insides of the chocolates. Of course, it can leave a fairly ugly box of evidence.
- You're eating the filling from the Oreos, but not the cookies. Once again, it doesn't count unless you eat the cookie and since they are easy to throw like little frisbees, the evidence can be disposed of quickly.
- You're having the occasional cracker because you "miss the crunch."
- You're putting cream and sugar in your coffee. As you know, a little cream and sugar can't hurt.

Create Your Own Emergency Response Plan

I know from personal experience that overcoming the temptation to comfort oneself with food is something that takes a considerable amount of time and commitment. In fact, even if your issue isn't so much related to temptation, the process of stopping yourself from reaching out to the foods that you have enjoyed in the past is not very easy.

So, for me, I always had an emergency plan in place. Meaning, I consciously decided that if I found myself opening the cabinets in the kitchen or staring in the fridge in a zombie-like fashion, then it was time to take action. When I started to act this way, I would immediately get in the car and go to the bookstore. For some reason, I have never had a problem getting lost in all the books and it always would take my mind off of whatever I was craving. And when the bookstore wasn't convenient at 2:00 a.m., then we never had a lack of folding clothes or cleaning. Bottom line, what allowed me to get past these moments wasn't the fact that I would look around for something to take my mind off of the temptations, but the fact that I already had a plan in place. So, in a way, I treated the moments of temptation and cravings the same way I would treat a fire. I immediately reacted and put a predefined plan into place. But instead of performing the old "stop, drop, and roll" or calling 911, I simply put my own emergency temptation and craving action plan into place. And, while I didn't have to do it often, it never failed to help.

. . . .

Draw the Line

I can remember driving home from work one evening when I started craving something to eat. While this wasn't very unusual, I realized that I was having the same craving each night at the same time. Specifically, the craving always hit on my way home from work and always whispered to me to stop at the same convenience store and pick up some survival goodies for the drive home. But, on this one night, something finally clicked. I realized that I wasn't hungry at all and that I was simply reacting to an old habit that I now needed to break.

Obviously, easier said then done, but simply being in the moment and being aware of what is going on is the first step. For me, when this craving hit, I decided it was time to draw the line in the sand. So, in doing so, I asked myself if I was committed to losing weight and creating a new lifestyle, or if I wanted to continue down the same old path?

And thank goodness the answer was no! As a result, I was able to get past the cravings and continue the course. In fact, by continuing to ask myself this hard question whenever faced with a temptation, it never ceased to allow me to take control of the moment and stick to the plan.

Unopened Jar of Peanut Butter

My wife and I have developed a great system to ensure that I'm successful on my program. Besides all of the obvious things, one of the key success factors for me is not bringing food in the house that may tempt me. Typically, this would include crackers, chips, chocolate, cookies, etc. I have absolutely no problem staying away from these foods when I'm not at home, but once in the house, I still have a tendency to graze in the kitchen.

We were shopping at our local grocery store and she decided that she wanted to get some peanut butter. Although I don't eat that stuff, I suggested she buy extra crunchy. Of course, she bought extra creamy (she's looking out for my best interests). To make matters worse, she bought the peanut butter and put it in the cabinet. The unopened jar of peanut butter has now been in the cabinet for over two weeks. So today, I asked her whether she was ever going to open the peanut butter and she said she actually just bought it because she knew that it would drive me nuts. Well, she was right. So, this lonely jar of unopened peanut butter has now become a symbol of my dedication. My wife thinks this is funny (she is right) and we have decided that if I can ever get to the point of looking in the cabinet without moving the unopened jar of peanut butter, then I will have reached a new milestone.

A Funny Night of Temptations with My Wife

While I'm not one to complain, I have to say that one night was extremely trying. Let me explain....

The fun started on my way home from work one night, when my wife called me and asked me to pick up some candy for her office on my way home. This was a very dangerous situation and I can assure you that in my previous life, I would have picked up one bag of candy for her office and one bag of candy to eat in the car on the way home. But I stuck to my guns, bought the candy, and successfully arrived home. Mission accomplished. Or, so I thought...

Upon my arrival home, my wife asked if I would make her something to eat. Absolutely no problem and I actually enjoy cooking. However, she requested that I make her a grilled cheese sandwich and some French bread pizza. This is not a typical meal in my home, but my wife was three weeks away from giving birth. I said of course, once again...In my previous life I would have made one sandwich for her and two for me, one pizza for her and two for me. But, once again, I survived the moment and enjoyed my evening supplement.

After dinner, my wife asked me to drive to Baskin Robbins and pick up a quart of Eggnog ice cream. I thought, surely, she must be trying to break me!! But, being a good husband, off I went. And, once again I successfully picked up the ice cream and arrived home without incident. It's situations like this, which not only test us, but truly allow us to evaluate the progress that we have made.

Eating Through Your Pets

Although it may be tempting to do, it's critical not to get caught into the habit of cooking for your friends and family for purely the enjoyment of eating vicariously through them. I can tell you from experience that whenever I felt like eating something, it would miraculously be served to the family for dinner that night. Of course, I wouldn't eat any of it, but the act of preparing it always fulfilled my cravings. However, while feeding friends and family might seem like fun, they unfortunately do not always want to eat what I was craving. But I do have a couple of house guests that never complain and are always up for a snack. You guessed it, the cat and dog. If I thought eating vicariously through friends and family was fun, the cat and dog always made for the most eager food recipients. For starters, the dog eats just about anything, which was always handy. No matter what I felt like cooking, the dog was always up for it and never complained. And, our cat has proved to be an equally helpful around the house. In fact, my wife had a habit of eating cheese at night. Since she doesn't have a weight problem, it was never a big deal for her, but it often caused me to have a few cravings. Thankfully, our cat often came to my rescue. If I felt like eating, I turned to the cat and simply gave her the food instead. Now, this is not to say that what I was feeding the dog or cat was the healthiest of foods, but when I had to get past the occasional craving, they certainly were always ready to help.

Busted By My Wife

Each morning and evening, I start and stop my day with the same routine—I have a cup of coffee. And I have always been a fan of sugar, but from dieting, have learned to use artificial sweeteners. I have for the most part stuck with using the sweeteners, but recently I started using real sugar in my tea. For me, this was not a big deal and definitely not a slippery slope item, but for my wife, it was a bad habit that needed to be nipped in the bud.

So, when I came home one day, she brought up the issue of the sugar vs. artificial sweetener and I said that using artificial sweetener was really not that big a deal. But she disagreed and made me promise that I would no longer put sugar in my coffee. "Yeah, yeah, no worries," was basically my reply.

On Friday morning, before leaving for work, I stopped in the kitchen and made a cup of coffee for the road. I decided to skip the Sweet N Low, and put a teaspoon of real sugar in my coffee. I usually have cell phones going off in the morning and I'm running late for one meeting or another, and I don't typically start drinking my coffee until I'm in my car and on the road. And Friday morning was no exception.

Unfortunately, about a block from my house, on a cell phone call, I took a huge gulp of my coffee. And, much to my surprise, the sugar that I thought I had put into my coffee was actually salt!!! Can you imagine how fast the realization of this situation brought the car to a screeching stop? I found myself gasping for water, and trying to figure out what happened. Then I started to laugh.

My wife had set me up, and what made it worse, I was the one that pulled the trigger! And, to add insult to injury, this very act would result in a victory dance by my wife and endless laughter for several days to come. This was definitely a fate worse than death, so I decided to keep this knowledge to myself. Of course, in sharing this experience in this book, I have no doubt that I have much dancing and laughing coming my way. So, should you see her, don't mention the coffee incident—our secret!

The Dreaded Mini-Bar

My wife and I were celebrating our 5th Wedding Anniversary and booked ourselves into a hotel in San Francisco for a couple of nights. It should have been a fun evening with lots of neat stuff, but little did I know that I would be facing my own personal diet kryptonite......The Dreaded Mini-Bar!!! Oh how I hate those things.

Whoever invented the mini-bar should be hunted down and forced to go on a diet. To me, it's like some sort of little torture machine that quietly sits in the room. Then, at about 2:00 a.m., it starts mocking and calling to me. So, in a purely defensive move, I got up, filled the garbage can in our room with its contents and sent it all down in the elevator to the lobby. Of course, doing this cost me about $200 bucks, but at least the front desk staff were happy to receive a late night snack. The following day, before heading out, I instructed the hotel front desk not to stock the mini-bar. And I was more than happy to pay for the previous night's elevator surprise, but I definitely didn't want to have a repeat performance.

You can imagine my surprise upon returning to our room and discovering that instead of an empty mini-bar, the staff had removed all of the items from the inside of the mini-bar and placed the contents in a basket next to our bed. This was definitely unfair, but desperate times call for desperate measures. To get the stuff away from me, I decided to lock the contents in the room safe. What is funny about this is that I was required to select a 4 digit code before placing the contents inside the safe. No problem...I punched a bunch of buttons at random, threw the goody basket inside the safe, with a note, and closed the door. Of course, I had no idea what the code was, so it was impossible for me to get the items out without a blow torch. Mission accomplished!

Reaching the "I Can Do This" Point!

It's different for each of us, but along the way you'll discover a point in the journey where you suddenly say, "Wow, I can do this. If I truly want to reach my goal weight and change my life forever then I have the power and all of the tools to make this happen."

It's an amazing feeling and for some of us it happens within the first 24 hours, by just discovering that we got through a day without dying—that it could be done. For others, it takes getting past the first week. For others, it's the first month. And for others, it's finally reaching a specific goal weight or getting through a hard challenge. As I said, the moment of truth for each of us is very different and it will often come when you least expect it. However, it's a very powerful thing.

I know for myself, being someone that had tried and failed 1000% on other approaches, when I finally came to the realization that I could do this, it was extremely empowering. And, for me, it had little to do with a time or a date and more to do with the understanding that I was getting my own behaviors under control. It was the fact that I was taking them seriously and allowing myself to learn that while I might not beat them overnight, I could learn how to manage them in the process.

Anyway, we each have a different point of discovery along the way and it's a personal moment that only you know about. But it's also a life changing one and in many ways is like standing in front of a cell door that was locked for many years, only to discover that it's now open and a very exciting life and world awaits you. And, while you may still have some work to do, you have now reached the glorious point in the process where you have the confidence in knowing that YOU CAN DO THIS.

Personal Ingredient 5: Listen to Your Body

Now having reached your fifth personal ingredient, it is time to learn how to listen to your body. And, for many people, the feeling of hunger is one of the loudest messages that we ever receive. When we feel hungry, our immediate reaction is to eat. So, it's important to first create a new relationship with how we view hunger and the issues that are making us feel that way.

Unfortunately, for many of us, hunger is linked with a number of different events in our lives. So, to break the link between the situations in our lives and the way we react to them, the following strategies have been put in place:

Remove the Temptations: One of the best ways to break the link between the sight of food and the response of hunger for that food is to remove it. If you are living with people that have tempting food in the house, try keeping it out of sight, in a specific drawer or pantry. Remember, when you are trying to get control over yourself, food control is critical. And, while it may seem extreme, often the best path for gaining control is removal.

Break the TV Cycle: For many of us, we are accustomed to eating each time we turn on the TV. Remember, if you are eating while you are watching TV, chances are you are completely unaware of this food trigger, and just how much food you are consuming. Make the decision to no longer eat and watch TV at the same time. This is a very difficult habit to break. But, in doing so, you'll find that your waistline will improve, and your relationship with your spouse, family, or friends will also improve.

Food is Not Your Friend: Most everyone with a weight issue reaches for comfort food when they feel empty, lonely, depressed, or bored. In the future, when you are feeling lonely, depressed, or bored, and experience the urge to eat, take this opportunity to better understand your own issues. Spend more time with family or friends. Take action on the issues that are causing you to seek comfort in food. And if you are bored, do something to entertain yourself without food.

As you can see, in learning how to control your appetite, you must learn how to become aware of foods that you are being exposed to, the impact of television, and your different moods and how they contribute to your eating. Remember, the more that you begin to understand the triggers that are impacting your appetite and overall hunger, the more you'll come to appreciate your body and how it utilizes food as fuel and not as a coping mechanism.

Chapter Six

Living in an Overweight Society

"Although the world is full of suffering, it is also full of overcoming it."

—Helen Keller

Recently, I had a really funny experience. I attended a morning conference where I was encouraged to arrive early. Not realizing why, I did as requested and was greeted and told that because of my early arrival, a free pre-conference breakfast was being provided. This seemed funny to me, but since I was a guest I smiled and went along with it.

The craziness didn't stop...

Throughout the morning conference, people would get up and walk out of the conference room and go to what they called break rooms, where a large selection of pastries and muffins was always available. Being a coffee drinker and totally bored by the conference, I inevitably found myself in one of the break rooms. I could not miss hearing the conversations on how people were enjoying the pastries and muffins and eating extra because it was free. Some attendees loaded their jacket pockets with free muffins and took the items back into the main conference room.

Fortunately, my speaking engagement was finished by noon, so I broke for the exit. Unfortunately, half way to the door, the conference broke for lunch and I soon found myself in a sea of people motivated by food, heading down the hall in search of lunch.

Thankfully, the exit door swung open and I was able to escape the insanity of the corporate feeding frenzy. As I walked to my car, I laughed. These were all employees of a single company, so no extra money had been paid for food. The more I thought about this, the more I realized that these people saw the food as a basic perk of the job. Just like their 401k, Health Benefits, Vacation, etc. I have no doubt that under any normal situation, none of these people would have overeaten, but when food was used as a perk, they wanted to make sure they got their fair share.

So, what does all this mean?

It means that you really need to be aware of what is going on. You need to understand that within a company, food is often used as a perk for employees. And whether it's as extreme as the eating at the conference I mentioned or as simple as an occasional birthday cake in the office, you have the power not to participate! Open your eyes and see how much of this goes on around you. The more you are aware of it, the more you'll be able to separate yourself from this craziness.

For those that are not in offices during the day, take the time to see how much of these same behaviors are used at social, community, civic, and within religious organizations. More often than not, to show appreciation for those that help in organizations, the payment often comes in the form of food.

I realize that the majority of food served to people is done as an act of kindness. But it's imperative for your own immediate and long-term success that you become very aware of these food moments around you. When you are ready, take the lead in changing your own world. If you have the opportunity to reward people within your own office or organization, step outside the box. Don't think with food, think with fun. Remember, you have the unique opportunity to change not only yourself, but also the world around you.

. . . .

Taking Off the Blinders

One of the most amazing things about going through the process of change and losing weight is that it provides a new start and a fresh perspective on life, both from the standpoint of allowing yourself to get back on track, and from the way you view the world. For me, in my heavy days, I thought nothing of going to drive-thru windows or enjoying restaurants without giving much thought as to what I was putting into my body.

Like a greyhound that has been spending its entire life chasing a bunny down the track, I found myself taking off the blinders and analyzing my old favorite places to eat, and I could see that they were slowly killing me!

This problem went far beyond the obvious fast food eatery. Like a victim re-approaching the scene of a crime, I began revisiting my old favorite restaurants and looking at the menus with fresh eyes. Specifically, I was looking for healthy lean meat and vegetable choices. Oh, big surprise, the results were very disturbing. I did find a few glimmers of hope. And, within a world of deep fried nonsense, I found restaurants that offered grilled meats, fish, and vegetables. I had to look and they were often few and far between, but those healthy eateries are there...

. . . .

Public vs. Private Reason for Losing Weight

When I'm asked what my biggest motivational factor was for losing weight, I have an answer for friends and family (public reason) and my own internal answer (private reason).

I typically tell everyone that I lost the weight because I want to be healthy and live a long time. This is true. However, my more immediate and most powerful motivating factor was that I wanted to look good again. To be brutally honest, I was tired of the implications that being overweight carried, tired of the looks, the "big guy" comments, and tired of having to shop at the Big Guy store.

So, while I lost the weight for health reasons (everyone loves that answer), my internal motivations were based mainly on vanity. And as a result, I feel better about myself. Now, don't get me wrong. I fully appreciate the health aspects of losing the weight and it wasn't until I hit my goal weight that I truly understood them. In fact, if I had known how much of my own life I saved, my motivations might have been different. However, I cannot deny the motivating power of vanity.

. . . .

Buying In Bulk

Prior to losing weight, one of the things that I used to love to do was shop at various wholesale membership clubs. As a result, I would buy foods in bulk and feel justified for doing it because of the cost savings.

For example, in our house we had three refrigerators. One was in the kitchen for general food, and two were in the garage for extras. One kept sodas and beer and the other one kept bulk food and cheeses. Looking back, I acted as if war could break out at any moment. We found we were getting better deals on food, but in quantities way beyond our needs. In addition, we bought food that was really bad for us. Everything from mini pizzas to 10 pound cheese blocks. We justified it all because we were getting a bargain, and with this bargain I got bigger and bigger. I decided to have a new mantra of quality over quantity. So, while I still shop at wholesale membership clubs, I now do it from the perspective of focusing only on the foods that fit my new lifestyle. And I have also changed our house to ensure that one refrigerator is enough.

Grocery Stores and Other Errands

In my former life, my wife used to think I was the most helpful guy in the world. Anytime she needed an errand run, I would be the first to volunteer. Of course, I wasn't doing it because I wanted to help, I was doing it as an excuse to be able to get out of the house and do a quick drive by at my favorite fast food outlet.

Even if the errand didn't take me past one of my favorite fast food venues, if I was going to the grocery store for milk, cheese, or bread, the chances were 100% that something else would end up in the cart and be eaten by the time I got home. I never really understood the extent of my problems until I was suddenly forced to face these issues...No more snacks on the run, no more late night drive through adventures.

I was caught off guard one night when my wife asked me to run down to the grocery store for milk. It seemed that almost the moment I got into my car; I started thinking about what I could buy and eat by the time I got home. I didn't act on it and I have no plans to ever let those impulses control my life again; however, I have come to the realization that these demons, while controllable, are definitely always lurking.

Season Weight Gains/Losses

If you are anything like me, this diet is probably not your first one. For me, I've been on just about every commercial diet available, and have also experienced a myriad of different successes and failures. In looking back, I probably would be classified as a classic yo-yo dieter. While I have spent countless hours trying to figure out why, I have come to the conclusion that much of my yo-yo behavior is probably due to sports. From grade school through college, I was encouraged to bulk up prior to the start of football season, and shed the weight when it was over. Of course, to do this meant eating large quantities of food (nothing I ever had a problem with). In looking back, I probably followed this cycle of weight gain/loss from the age of 10 through 22. And while it seemed perfectly normal at the time, the ramifications of this behavior are now obvious.

After school, when I began working in corporate America, I had the hardest time breaking this behavior. No matter what I did, I seemed programmed to think that the fall stood for bulking up and the spring stood for weight loss. For years, I continued to pack on 50 pounds in September/October, only to drop it again the following March/April. And then, something very odd happened. My metabolism started to slow down. And little by little I started keeping some of the weight on each season. As a result, the spring ritual of weight loss became a yearly nightmare. In fact, it became so difficult, I decided that instead of bulking up and slimming down each year, it would be much easier to just stay in game shape (overweight) the entire year round. Yep, that was much easier and somehow or another I convinced myself that this was all right.

Of course, as all of us know, it doesn't take long to realize the social and physical ramifications of being overweight. Thus, I started my transition to becoming an "adult dieter." However, having entered the corporate world, my weight gain was no longer referred to as my "game weight," but now referred to as "my winter coat." Of course, these were all just semantics, and the fact remained that I was still gaining and losing weight each year.

Unfortunately, one can only play this game for so long. And the older I got, the more this strategy fell apart. In fact, it wasn't too long before my wife pointed out to me one Sunday that I was heavier than anyone on the front line of the Oakland Raiders. At first, this sounded fantastic. But I quickly remembered that I didn't have a million dollar football contract. And, unfortunately, the closest I'd ever get to being an Oakland Raider was when I passed the coliseum on the train to work.

Surviving County Fairs and Art/Wine Festivals

During the summer, my wife and I enjoy going to County Fairs and Art/Wine Festivals. However, over the years, I have noticed a disturbing trend towards some of the things that are being served. Specifically, would you believe that they are now deep frying Twinkies and Oreo Cookies? Now, I don't have a problem with the majority of foods that people eat, but some things are just crossing the line.

In the past, going to a fair or art and wine festival was always just an excuse to eat my way through the event. Now, I find myself actually looking at the exhibits and taking my time to find the things that are refreshing and still good for me. It has definitely thrown a new twist into the events, but all for the better. This just goes to show that even in the places where we committed our most outrageous crimes of caloric consumption, we can be victorious.

Plus Size Clothing for Men and Women

If you haven't noticed already, within our society is forming a very unhealthy acceptance of being overweight. I don't mean this from the perspective of supporting and understanding those that are overweight, but from the commercial aspect of companies that are promoting an overweight lifestyle. Now, don't get me wrong, when I was a larger person it was next to impossible to find anything of any style that I actually wanted to be seen in. So, in having the option of shopping at a store that served the fashion needs of a larger person, I was grateful. But what I have found to be very annoying is that some of these stores are trying to show that being a larger person is something to be proud of. They actually promote being big as a badge of honor, while completely ignoring the obvious health impacts. Sadly, these promotions are working and more and more people are accepting being big as a way of life. But trust me, being a "Big Dog" for life is nothing to be proud of.

Of course, on the flip side, some of the more responsible plus size clothing stores are also very active in promoting health and fitness for the larger person. So, as you are losing the weight and getting into shape, be conscious of where you are shopping and the messages that are being put in front of you. Seek out the places that promote health and fitness and know that while you may be a large, you are really just in a transition period where you will soon be sleek and sexy.

. . . .

Revenge of the Girl Scout Cookies

I had thought that Girl Scout cookie season was well past us, but I found out just the opposite one day. While I was visiting my God children, they reminded me that I had ordered 10 boxes of thin mint cookies in September. As a general rule, I would buy the cookies to help the children out, and then my wife would take the cookies into the office. However, I had not been out to see them in a few months, hence the cookie backlog. When I left, my God Daughter gave me the boxes of cookies. Typically, this wouldn't be a problem, but with an hour drive back to my house, the cookies seemed to be calling me. I was 10 minutes down the road when I felt the old thoughts start to come back into my mind. It's really amazing how some demons just don't want to die.

I pulled over to the nearest 7-11, loaded up on coffee, and left the neighborhood bum with enough cookies to last him through the summer (at least someone is enjoying them). I wouldn't think that this would have been a problem, but for some reason, having the cookies in the seat next to me just proved too tempting to resist. When I got home, the kids called and asked my wife if she got the cookies. You can imagine her surprise. "What cookies?" she asked, as I walked into the house. While I felt silly having to explain myself, it certainly was better than the alternative of breaking into the cookies.

Personal Ingredient 6: Recognizing Stress

As we all know, stress is an unavoidable factor of life. However, having too much stress in our lives can interfere with our ability to function correctly or make healthy decisions. People run into problems with their weight, when they turn to food as a means of coping with their stress. Therefore, it's very important to learn how to recognize the things that cause you stress, and how to effectively react to them, without turning to food. As a result, with your sixth personal ingredient, you'll learn how to identify your personal areas of stress and how to manage them, without turning to food.

In order to get a handle on your stress, it's critical to come to terms with the things in your life that cause you stress. Now begin the process by identifying the stress causers. Take a moment and list out the various things that cause you the most stress in your life (money, family, house work, etc.). Review your list and consider the things that are causing you to have an increase in appetite or food cravings. It is quite common to respond to stress with the comfort of food.

In creating your list, it is important to become aware of what is happening in your life and the impacts that stress can have on your waistline. In doing this, you can then move forward with a better understanding of how you've reacted to stress in the past, and how you will choose to react to stress in the future. Being aware of your personal coping methods and a willingness to change are the most important keys to success. Obviously, this exercise is not something that you can do in just a single sitting. So, make it a goal to create your list over the next several days and really take the time to get a true understanding of the causes of stress in your life, and most importantly, how they have impacted your weight up to this point in your life.

Chapter Seven

Family & Friends

"Lots of people want to ride with you in the limo, but what you want is someone who will take the bus with you when the limo breaks down."

— Oprah Winfrey

I'm lucky to have a very loving and supportive wife, but my weight and eating issues always confused her. In fact, since she is someone that has never had weight issues, she has never been able to understand my weight problem. I can remember a time she was so confused by the weight gain and she had tried just about every approach to get me to do something about it until one evening in 2002 when she sat me down and said:

"I love you, but I didn't sign up for what you have done to yourself. When we met, you looked different and over the years you have changed. I'm certainly not leaving you, but please let me know if this is going to be the way things are, then I'll accept it and stop trying or caring so much."

This was a stark reminder of how what I had done to myself was not only impacting me, but also my loved ones.

Consider the Impacts on Those Around You

Life is very hard and each of us has had our share of getting knocked around and being forced to get back up. In fact, as we get older, many people often give up on their goals and dreams. It's not a matter of no longer wanting to achieve their goals, but rather fear of failure that often leads us to complacency with life.

Having said this…consider the impact of your success on those around you! Think about it. You are a person that has stood up in the crowd and decided that you are not going to settle for second best, that life is too short to accept anything but success. And as you move forward and achieve success, you are not only proving this to yourself, but to those around you. I know it may sound like a small thing, but the more successful you are, the more of an impact you will have on your friends and family. Specifically, people will begin to view what you have accomplished as a call to duty on their own dreams and goals. Because, if you can do it, so can they. For many people this might mean:

- Writing the book they always wanted to write
- Getting back into their artwork
- Pursuing their education
- Getting new professional skills
- Getting back into dancing
- Getting back into sports
- Starting their singing again
- Playing with the kids or grandkids like never before
- Traveling in comfort and seeing the world

- Getting in touch with old friends and getting social again

Remember you are someone who is standing up in a sea of people and you may find that you are the catalyst for others around you to do the same.

. . . .

Friends and Their Eating

Ever since I was a little kid, I had an amazing ability to eat. And with that came the obvious result of being a bigger kid than most. I didn't have much fun in grade school, but as I became more active in high school, I found that things evened themselves out. I have always been somewhat burdened or blessed (depending on your perspective) with the ability to gain size very quickly. Obviously, a benefit when I played sports, but in real life, more of a burden.

In observing friends over the years, I have noticed the following three types of eating:

The Eaters: These are the people that have naturally fast metabolisms and can generally eat whatever they want without gaining any weight. Typically, they are smaller framed people who also have a very hard time putting on muscle.

The Moderators: These are the people that have the amazing ability to keep themselves in check at all times. They never seem to overeat and don't seem very involved in food. It almost appears that eating is an inconvenience to their day.

The Fitness Kings and Queens: These are the people who appear to be able to eat whatever they want, but in reality are working out several hours a day.

I know for a great many years, I thought I was the only one that was cursed with eating too much. And I often found myself jealous of the way my friends could seemingly eat anything. But the truth is that each person is very different in how they handle their relationship with food. I have finally come to appreciate my unique background and how it has allowed me to have a better balance and perspective about my friends and eating.

Consider the Power of Putting Yourself First

One of the most common traits shared by many dieters is the position of supporter or caregiver for others.

A support position creates an environment of putting other people's needs before your own. And, while we may not mean to do it, what often happens is that we sacrifice the time required for us to take care of ourselves.

I'm not saying that helping and supporting family and friends shouldn't continue, only that a happy middle ground needs to be found. If you are a person who has always put others before yourself, you may find that your diet or the time you require to exercise is a little threatening to those around you.

While it may be hard, positively stand your ground and make time for yourself. If those around you have a hard time with this, well, they'll just have to learn to deal with it. Remember, nothing is more important than the process that you are going through, not only from the perspective of losing weight, but from the perspective of life style changes.

If you have been having a hard time with this issue, know that putting yourself first isn't a bad thing. You may just find that in doing this; you set an example for the family, and begin to re-establish balance in other areas of your life as well.

Husband and Wife Confusion

One of the hardest situations to be in is to be married to someone who does not share your same problem with eating or having a weight issue. Sure, it's great that you aren't sitting around enabling each other, but the true problem with this dynamic is that it's almost impossible to describe to the other person the issues that you have, if they are completely unable to relate to them. For example, my wife would often get extremely frustrated with me regarding my weight gain. Out of frustration, she would often remind me that I no longer looked like the person that she married. Furthermore, she would rub salt into the wound by asking me if I would like to be seen in public with her, if she had put on the same amount of weight that I had. Obviously, these were real frustrations that she was having with me and without having any concept of the issues that I was going through or trying to overcome, all she could do was try and put me in her situation. But, as you can imagine, although I certainly empathized with her and agreed with everything that she was saying, none of these truths were the key to allowing me to overcome my own issues. In fact, the more pressure that she applied, the harder it actually became to take action. And being someone that didn't like confrontation, I would just agree with her to allow her to get the issues off her chest, and then leave the house angry with myself for the situation that I had created. Unfortunately, not having the skills at the time to overcome my own problems, I would then turn to the only support system that I had—food!!

Of course, while hunkered over a tray full of Taco Bell, I would then mumble and grumble to myself over the issue. And, instead of getting angry at the problem and the control that food had created in my life, I would instead get angry at my wife. This would then lead me to thoughts like, "I'll show her." Munch, munch, munch…

"How dare she tell me that I shouldn't eat anymore." Munch, munch, munch..."I'm not hungry, but I'm going to eat anyways, just to show her who is boss." Munch, munch, munch...

And thus, the insanity continued. For me, I was ultimately not able to truly stop getting angry with my wife over this issue, until I was able to come to peace with the fact that she truly had no concept as to my own issues with food or eating. A great analogy is that I have no concept as to what it is like to have a taste for alcohol. Yes, I enjoy the occasional drink, but I really have no craving for it. As a result, while I might be able to understand the cravings that an alcoholic has, I truly have no concept since I don't walk in that person's shoes. So, in seeing how my wife could not possibly understand what was going on with me or with the issues I was facing, I came to peace with the situation. I stopped getting frustrated with her lack of understanding and I turned my frustration inwards and began attacking the true problem—the control that food was having over my life. In doing so, I took the time to explain these things to my wife. I gave her the benefit of the doubt along the entire journey and while I knew that she would truly never understand me, I made the decision to make her a part of the solution, instead of a part of the problem. As a result, she backed off her comments, started to become more supportive, and gave me the space to work through the issues.

Although losing the weight and creating a new lifestyle is something that you must do for yourself, it's critical to make your partner part of the journey. Ultimately, you are taking back your life, while creating a new one and nothing is more rewarding than knowing that you are not only doing it as a team, but that you'll both be reaping the benefits together.

Kids

Kids certainly enrich our lives and make us complete, but they also cause an entirely different level of stress and anxiety in our lives. I know for myself, its one thing to worry about your career and the typical problems of life, but when you add kids into the mix, it creates an entirely new perspective on one's own priorities. Suddenly, the things that once seemed so important, like diet and exercise, are replaced with huge financial responsibilities and a seemingly endless life of no sleep, cleaning-up the house, baths, bedtime stories, and constant supervision. It's absolutely no wonder why most people that have kids fall into the trap of putting on weight and not exercising. Amazingly, at a time in our lives when our kids need us to be healthy the most, it's easy to justify not going to the gym or picking up food on the way home, instead of taking the time to cook something healthy.

I'm not saying that children should not be a parent's number one priority, I'm just saying that if you are a parent, you should view your job in life as not only being a provider, but also an example of how to live. Remember, your kids will watch and emulate your every move and if they don't see you exercising or taking care of yourself, they won't either. And if they don't see you eating healthy, then you can be assured that they'll also copy these habits.

Now, here is the good news.

Whether your kids are newborns, 10 years old, or 30 years old, you will never stop being an example to them. And whether or not you have lived your life in a way that you now regret, it's never too late to show them that you can change your ways. In fact, while it's great to raise your kids in an environment that stresses healthy eating and fitness, it's even more powerful if you can show your adult children that it's never too late to take your life back. In doing so, you are not only re-establishing a new life for yourself, but also giving your kids the invaluable lesson of knowing that it's never too late to live your life to its fullest: "If Mom and Dad can change, then I can change too!"

. . . .

Starting New Family Traditions

If you are anything like me, the majority of your family holiday traditions are centered on food. Whether they are a special dish, dessert, or drink, most of my family traditions are related to food. I wanted to break the chain of overweight men in my family, and I decided that it was time to start some new traditions. For example, while our family and friends will always have great food traditions around our house, I also wanted to create new holiday traditions that are not food related. This way, as my children grow up, their memories will not be centered on food and eating, but the fun things that we did as a family. And, as hard as this may be, the buck starts with me.

Some of our family traditions now include:

- Enjoying walks on holidays like Thanksgiving, Christmas Eve, and Christmas Morning.
- Enjoying sledding or skiing with the family at Lake Tahoe and staying out of the casino buffet.
- Ending each day with a walk in the evening.
- Going out to the movies or the theatre with the family and not having to go to dinner first.
- Starting Saturday or Sunday mornings by going for a walk.
- Hanging out with the family at the hotel pool in Vegas and staying out of the casino buffet (notice a trend?).

- Checking out the local farmers market on the weekends and trying new things.

Eating Buddies

If you are anything like me, much of your social life was centered on food. I know for myself, I had an entirely different set of friends for each meal. I had one friend that I always met for breakfast. I had a lunch group at work. And I had another group of friends for trying new restaurants. I had bar eating friends too.

When I started my diet, it was truly eye opening. For the first time, I had to approach my social eating friends and explain to them that I was taking a break from all eating activities. Some of my friends were very excited for me, and others acted like someone had died.

The more time passed, the more I came to understand that many of my friends were only eating buddies and now that I was dieting, we had nothing in common. This was a harsh wake-up call and an unexpected result of the diet.

Overweight Friends

One of the most interesting things that I discovered while I was losing weight was that my enthusiasm for the program continued to increase. It was an amazing thing, since I'm just a regular guy who had 100 pounds to lose. I couldn't help but think that if I was successful on the program, then anyone could be. Well, much to my surprise, I found that the biggest opponents I ran into while on the diet were other people that were overweight. My friends that were thin were amazingly encouraging and those that were overweight tried to discourage me at every bend. It seemed that my overweight friends wanted me to fail. In fact, the common response I received from people while on the diet was, "Well, you're doing well now, but what happens when you get off the diet?" I always had the same answer: "Who cares?"

I discovered that many people had given up on the thought that they could be thin again and accepted the state they were in. And, since misery loves company, I shouldn't fight them, but join the Bon Bon club. I wasn't some kind of diet cheerleader encouraging everyone to participate, but when you're dropping 5-7 pounds a week, you become a walking billboard. In fact, I have a few friends that didn't even want to see me anymore. My success seemed to remind them of something they needed to do. You can lead a horse to water, but you can't make it drink. I learned to keep my mouth shut and continue on my program. In fact, when people would inquire as to what I was doing to lose all the weight, I had a tendency to downplay the diet so as to not offend anyone in the vicinity that might be of a larger stature. I watched a program with a group of large people on it who claimed they were happy with their appearance. I found this very hard to believe. For starters, if you are a bigger person it's hard to find a car that is comfortable, it's hard to fly, clothes are limiting, you are always hot, always thirsty, it's hard to walk up stairs, sports are out of the question, and if you're single—it's even harder to meet people. I think for many, it's just too hard to lose the weight and probably much easier to accept the circumstances. However, when you've been 100 pounds overweight and have come through the other end of the tunnel, you really do want everyone to have that same opportunity.

Negative Feedback from Family and Friends

We all talk about failure on our diets. I want to take a moment and share another perceptive on the subject and address the issue of negative feedback and success. While failure is certainly a scary thing, it can also be extremely valuable and can ultimately be the foundation of your success. Most of our fears are a direct result of our past experiences. If we have failed at a diet in the past or successfully lost weight only to put it back on again, the fear of failure is undeniably a reality. Try to view your past experiences from a new perspective. For example:

- The more that one fails, the more a person actually succeeds. Failure is really just a part of the process to get to a point where you can apply the past lessons to your future success. Failure can be a tool to help you examine yourself. Failure is where the changes need to occur in your life.

- There are only two ways of failing. One is by not trying and the other is by quitting. If you are reading this, neither of those applies to you.

- If you have failed in the past and now find yourself here today, what you have actually provided yourself with is the opportunity to apply a new solution.

Now, as anyone on a diet knows, you are going to be faced with negative feedback from family, friends and strangers, from people that don't understand what having a weight issue is like, from people that are threatened by your success, and from people that are just badly informed on the subject of dieting. Try to remember the following:

- If the feedback is invalid, don't take it personally.

- Your self-esteem and the vision of what is ahead of you are not dependent on the reactions or thoughts of others.

Never forget these three rules!!!!

1. Our beliefs affect our attitude.
2. Our attitude affects our performance.
3. Our performance determines our results!!

. . . .

Friends and Athletes

One of the most amazing admirable characteristics that I see in so many of my friends is their ability to be nostalgic and reminisce about the "good old days." In fact, my friend Bill (whom I have known since kindergarten) is especially fond of doing this and he never ceases to bring a smile to my face. Unfortunately, Bill also shares the characteristic of many former athletes. Being someone that was at the top of his own sport at a younger age, Bill came to the realization at some point that with age and time he would never be able to compete at the same level again. And, with the added responsibilities of marriage and kids, his priorities shifted and he came to accept his life as an athlete as a thing of the past. However, where most people would continue working out to stay in shape and be healthy, this notion is especially hard for former athletes. Unfortunately, for people like this, working out was never something that was seen as exercise, but as a part of a sport. So, when athletes retire or stop competing, they often find it hard to grasp the concept of going to the gym for exercise. Unfortunately, when they step into a gym setting, the old smells and sounds come back and they immediately want to compete again and return to their sport of choice. However, father time has taken this option away and they must then cross the critical hurdle of changing their mindset and re-approaching the gym from the perspective of health and fitness.

If you are a former athlete who is going through this challenge, then this is something that is critical to think about. It's critical to break the relationship between your sport and being fit. To appreciate all that you have in life and to recognize that while you may never compete at the same level again, you can at least be an athlete in how you approach your own personal health and fitness each day. And the worse shape you are in, the bigger the game ahead. Additionally, if you're a friend or family member of a former athlete who has seemingly lost their way, take the time to talk to them about how they view the gym and exercise in general. Unfortunately, while their perspective may seem warped, it is very real and the more you can assist them in coming to terms with it, the more they can begin the process of taking back their lives.

With regards to my friend Bill, it took him many years to transition from being an athlete to just a regular guy at the gym, but he did do it. And the good news is that he took his family along for the ride. So, instead of exercising alone, he took his daughters and wife with him, and as a result, they are now a very fit and happy family.

Confess to a Family Member

For me, one of my final steps in overcoming my eating issues was to confess some of my biggest secrets to my wife. Of course, what was especially hard about doing this was that when you are used to eating in a secret manner, it's very difficult to not only admit it to yourself, but then go one step further and admit it to someone close to you. Trust me; the vulnerability of the moment can be very intense, but also very rewarding.

If I had to label myself, I would have said that I was the classic closet eater. No, this doesn't mean I would eat in the closet, but I did do most of my eating on my own. If I was running errands, one of the errands would always include a drive through for a quick snack. And what was really scary was unless you were hiding in the trunk of my car, it appeared that I ate like everyone else. I was very good at eating in secret.

Now, here is the really funny part. As I progressed on my diet and left this life of closet eating behind, I never really addressed the snacking issue. Sure, I had been 100 pounds overweight, but it couldn't have had anything to do with my snacking. Could it?

Take a trip down memory lane with me.... One night, I found myself driving around town and doing some errands with my wife. We got on a conversation about eating behaviors and how I really didn't have any. So I decided to confess my former eating ways to my wife. Mind you, these were dark secrets that I shared with no one. So, we were in the parking lot of Home Depot, I began my confession...(Try not to laugh)

I told my wife about my eating alone. Not the kind of eating where I would stuff myself, but the kind of secret eating where I would graze from one food to another. I gave her the best example I could think of...my top secret trips to the grocery store. I told her that the quick trips for milk and bread were really an under-cover operation for my secret snacking. I would make an immediate stop at the in-store Deli. At this venue, I would load up on my favorite rations. Typically, this would include pot stickers or spring rolls; nothing heavy...since I needed to maintain a low eating profile. Then, I would cruise through the bakery and grab a couple of the free cookies that are always left on the counter for the kids. Of course, if they didn't have any cookies, I would be obliged to assist them and open a box or two. And, as if that wasn't enough, I would keep a look out for the little old ladies offering the free samples. In fact, after a while, we all knew each other by name. And let's not forget about the long drive home. Seeing as it was a journey of an incredible 5 blocks via the SUV, no trip would be complete without opening a box of cookies or crackers to ensure my survival.

So, there I was, sitting in the parking lot of Home Depot...giving my eating confession to my wife, and, amazingly, two things happened:

- First, we both laughed so hard that we ended up with tears running down our faces. She couldn't believe it!! But since I was obviously confessing my secret eating, it had to be true. And she had always wondered how I got so big when I ate so little at home.
- Hearing myself explain my past behaviors made me appreciate how crazy it must have sounded and only further helped me to face the issues.

So, while taking the step of confessing your behaviors to someone who is close to you might seem very scary, I can tell you that it not only did worlds for helping me to further overcome my issues, but also allowed my wife to better understand me. And as anyone knows who has friends or family members that don't have any eating or weight issues, nothing can be more confusing to them than trying to understand what it is you are going through. So, take the leap of faith and have the confidence in knowing that if you are loved by those around you, taking the time to bring them closer into your world will only strengthen the bonds that you already have.

Personal Ingredient 7: Your Inner Voice

In looking at your seventh personal ingredient, we are going to further discuss strategies for stress management. And if you are like most, you are asking yourself the following question: What does all this have to do with losing weight?

The answer is…Everything!!

Remember, one of the corner stones to creating a healthy new lifestyle is having a successful strategy for stress management. That means, when you practice good eating habits, use alcohol moderately or not at all, don't smoke and exercise regularly, you are better able to resist the physical and mental impacts of stress. Or, as it relates to weight loss, you'll be able to learn how to stop turning to food for comfort in times of stress.

To combat stress, you already have one of the most amazing tools—your inner voice! While you may not realize it, we each have an inner voice that we use each day. Typically, we use our inner voice to express our thoughts, or think about the things we wish we could say, but socially know are unacceptable. But when it comes to food or exercise, our inner voice can fail us. It is important to examine the power of our inner voice.

Have you ever said the following things to yourself?

"Diets don't work for me."

"If I lose weight, I'll just regain it."

"I can't live without chocolate."

"I'm too old to get my body back."

"I hate exercising."

"I don't like my diet…I can't do it."

"It's physically impossible for me to be lean."

"I have far too many social obligations to go on a diet."

"My life is too busy with my kids to allow me to lose weight."

"I'm too busy to exercise."

As you can see, negative statements are very powerful. The more we repeat negatives to ourselves, the more they become a reality. It's safe to say that every diet that ever failed started with a negative statement from within. However, our inner voice also has the power to make positive statements. And just like negative statements, the more we repeat positives, the more they become a reality. Remember, within each of us is an inner voice with the power to undermine our actions or strengthen them. Of course, the choice belongs to you!

In creating your new lifestyle, your goal is to monitor your inner voice and to take steps towards changing your negative thoughts into positive ones. Trust me on this; it's going to make a huge difference in your weight loss! So, let's start...As you go about your day-to-day business, listen to what you say to yourself. And as your thoughts come into your mind, write down the negative ones. Now, as you end the day having written down your negative thoughts, take a moment and review your list. In fact, make this an exercise that you do each day. And as you review your list, think about other ways to say the same thing. For example, instead of saying, "I can't do this diet, it's too hard," you could say, "This diet might be hard, but I can do this!" Or, instead of saying, "I'll start dieting or exercising on Monday," you could say, "Now is the time!"

Now, start the process of becoming aware of your inner voice and come to terms with the power of changing your thoughts. Remember, this is not an easy process, so for the time being, you'll have to be very conscious of what it is you are thinking. Then as you improve on the process you'll be able to reverse your inner voice to positive thoughts.

Change starts by taking the time to be aware of your inner voice, writing down your thoughts, and slowly creating a new voice for yourself. Remember, we are often our own worst enemies when it comes to dieting and creating change, so make it a point to become your own champion and start breaking the cycle of your inner voice. Have no doubt, this will require practice, so keep doing it over and over, and never forget that you are absolutely worth it and that these changes will greatly influence your weight loss.

Chapter Eight

Masking Our Emotions

"The same fence that shuts others out shuts you in."
—Bill Copeland

I think that one of the hardest things about being on a diet is coming to terms with how much we use food to mask our feelings. It's probably the most powerful drug available to man and the most widely used. If I use myself as an example, my weekly struggles seemed to be centered on work.

When I was my heaviest, I couldn't say that I loved my job, but it did pay the bills. With that said, my issues typically began on Sunday night. With the impending thought of starting another week of fun at the office, I would medicate myself by going out to dinner or having a big dinner at home. In the morning, I would mask the grumbling of entering cube city with a few donuts and a cup of coffee. Thank God for lunch, because if I couldn't escape the office for a mid-day Chinese food rendezvous, I don't think I could get through the madness. The afternoons were usually slow, but the office vending machine never failed to offer a little sanctuary. Coming home at the end of the day and having dinner with the family always helped to keep things in check. But, in thinking about the madness starting again the next day, a bowl of ice cream in bed never ceased to offer some late night solace. But, no matter what I ate, the Monday through Friday grind would repeat itself.

Now came the weekend. It would be great if I could say that I behaved on the weekend, but the truth is that things would get worse. I lived through the mantra, "Eat, live, and be merry, for on Monday I need to re-enter the office." It seemed that the more miserable I was at work, the more weight I would gain. Unfortunately, if things were so simple as to only be related to work, I could just get a better job and be thin again. If this were the case, I certainly would have done it. As many of you know, this behavior goes one step further...For example, if food worked so well to mask my feelings about work, why not apply the same medication to the other areas in my life? If I had a fight with my wife, eat a Snickers bar. Food always provided the perfect consolation prize. I always felt rewarded, it always tasted great, and it never talked back. Could I ask for a more perfect companion? In fact, food would be the perfect answer to most of my problems but, there's one huge side effect.... Weight gain!!!! It wasn't until I went on my diet, that the real problems in my life floated to the surface...Reality comes crashing in when you no longer have your drug of choice to turn too. By taking food out of the picture, I was forced to face my problems and issues... First off, this sucks!!! I never realized how happy candy made me, until it was taken away. What a bummer!!! Also, when food is taken out of the picture, every issue that would have been fixed by my crutch food seemed to be magnified 100 times. If I just had a Snickers bar to help me through this situation, life would be so much easier. Take away my food and you take away my happiness. At least, this is how it felt.

As for me, giving up the foods I loved was a life changing experience. All of a sudden, I had to make myself happy through other avenues and face issues without medication.

Excuses for Eating and Getting Caught

While I loved losing weight, the true benefit for me was attaining the feeling that I had control over my eating. Prior to starting my diet, I felt that every day was a struggle and while I started each Monday with a renewed sense of enthusiasm towards gaining control of my eating, I was never strong enough to do it.

This sense of being out of control was absolutely horrifying. And it was not until I started my diet that I felt that I had control again. Sure, the demons were always present, but as long as I stuck with the program, I no longer had the feeling of going to bed stuffed or waking up in the morning trying to stop myself from overeating and destroying another well intentioned day. Of course, now that I'm controlling my eating, as opposed to the other way around, it's easy to look back on some of my more sneaky behaviors. In fact, it's safe to say that I was a pro when it came to coming up with excuses for sneaking food, and the following are some of my favorites:

"I saw myself as quality control for the bakery, deli, and the Chinese food area at the grocery store. And I was always glad to report that they were doing a good job."

"It's a crime to drink coffee without chips and a sandwich. In fact, no beverage should be consumed without something to eat with it."

"If a man is expected to pick up Chinese food or Pizza on the way home, then it's critical that he also picks up egg rolls or chicken wings for the ride home."

"Nothing says I love you to my wife more than offering to get her a snack at night when she's in bed. Of course, this is also the perfect opportunity to enjoy a snack in the kitchen by myself."

And when I got caught, the following were my favorite excuses for explaining the evidence:

"Those aren't chips down the front of my shirt, I was trying a free sample at the grocery store and I must have spilled a few on myself."

"Those aren't my empty wrappers in the car. I was driving the guys to a meeting today and they left their stuff behind."

"I didn't finish the ice cream. It had freezer burn so I tossed it out."

"What do you mean two orders of egg rolls on the bill? We only had one!! Perhaps, they shorted us an order again. I'll talk to them later. But no way I'm driving back down and complaining about it tonight."

"No, those plates in the sink don't mean I've already eaten. I've been waiting for you to get home."

Trust me, my list goes on and on and I definitely had more than my fair share of excuses to eat and ready excuses to explain the evidence away. But in keeping a sense of humor and seeing the funny side of the things that I did, it truly helped me to approach the issues in a non-threatening manner. So, in looking at your own behaviors, start with the things that make you laugh the most, and the more progress you make in overcoming them, the more you'll be able to look back and not only see them as a thing of the past, but appreciate your new abilities in overcoming them.

. . . .

Confronting Your Inner Dialogue

While dieting, it is important to overcome your "inner dialogue." We all have self-statements that we say to ourselves throughout the day that cause us to take or not take action. Our "inner dialogue" is an amazingly powerful tool. And so, if our "inner dialogue" is negative, it can negatively impact us. This can be especially true when you are dieting. For example, have you ever said the following statements to yourself?

"I'll never be able to lose weight."

"These snacks are my favorite; I can't resist them."

"I look like a fool when I exercise...I won't do it."

"I don't like the taste of the supplement...I can't do this."

These are all classic examples of negative self-statements that can severely impact your weight loss efforts. Surprisingly, all failed diets can be traced back to someone starting with negative thoughts.

Eating Issues and Self Awareness

When I first started my diet my entire focus was on how much weight I could lose and how fast I could lose it. In fact, I would very carefully look at my weight each week and map out the length of time that I thought it would take me to reach my goal.

I lost the first 50-75 pounds with this attitude. I believe it was around the third month on the program, something finally clicked. I came to the realization that while I thought my journey would be over when I reached my goal weight, the reality was that it had only just begun. Sure, I was losing the weight and I would soon be reaching my goal, but what was stopping me from putting on the weight again?

This question haunted me...Why would I be any different from so many other people that have lost weight dieting, only to find themselves putting it right back on? Unfortunately, I did not have an answer.

I found myself saying things like...

"After this diet, I could live on grapes."

Or, my personal favorite,

"I'll worry about that problem when I reach my goal weight."

The answer is not very simple. For me, it started with an understanding that I have a problem with food. While it seems obvious, it's often too easy to blame our weight issues on external factors (stress, family, jobs, health, kids, etc.). I have no excuse but to say that I like to eat and I turn to food for many reasons, especially comfort. Somehow food became a close friend and one that I turned to often.

In examining myself, I was able to make peace with my own eating issues. As a result, I no longer saw the diet as a means to an end, but more as a means to learning how to live my life without eating issues. While I still maintained goals for myself and eagerly waited to reach my goal weight, I now saw my diet and progress as something far beyond the process of losing my weight. I saw the diet as a mechanism and a tool for learning new behaviors and preparing me for my new life ahead. I understand that my issues with eating will not go away, but now I'm able to see the big picture and help myself.

Ask yourself....Why is this time different? Why will I be able to keep the weight off? Perhaps the answer lies with your ability to admit that you have a problem that's not going away as soon as you reach your goal weight and is something that you must learn to deal with on a daily basis, for the rest of your life. By doing this, your journey not only becomes a path to reach your goal weight, but a journey to learn to live with your eating issues and still live a long, happy, and healthy life.

Becoming Self Aware

No one really sees how they look to others. For instance, I can remember when I was 300+ pounds, if I saw another man that was bigger than me, I would say something to my wife like, "Would you look at the size of that monster." She would typically respond, "You should keep your mouth shut, because you're not too much smaller than he is." The funny thing is that she was right. Even though I could not deny my size, my self-image was completely distorted from the reality of what I looked like. The good news was that I had a good self-image; the bad news was that I was kidding myself.

In fact, it wasn't until I looked at some pictures, that I realized the problem. I remember being so surprised by how I looked that I turned to my wife and asked if I really looked like this. Unfortunately, I was eating a cookie at the time and she laughed so hard that she couldn't answer. I guess that was answer enough. Coming to terms with my own size was one of the keys to getting started. Ultimately, seeing myself in the pictures was just too huge to ignore. I got the message and started my journey.

Personal Ingredient 8: Say Something Positive

Moving ahead with your eighth personal ingredient, we are now going to focus on allowing you to create truthful and positive statements about yourself. Learning how to do this and putting it into practice is extremely powerful and will greatly influence your behavior and the world around you. As an example, consider the following statements:

"Now is the time to change my life."

"I'm putting myself first."

"No one can stop me from being successful."

"I'm doing this for me."

"I'm taking my life back."

"Life is too short to not enjoy my body to its fullest."

"I want to be active and enjoy all that life has to offer."

Remember, what we are focusing on is not just overcoming negative thoughts, but more specifically, saying something positive about yourself and what it is you are doing!! Keep in mind, this is extremely powerful, and for many people, their weight issue can often be attributed to negative thinking. So, let's start with positive thinking right now!!

Think about the positive things that you can say to yourself throughout the day. If possible, try and come up with two or three positive statements. Now, having done this, repeat them again and again. Make them a part of your positive personal ingredients that you turn to in everything that you do. Apply them when you face any situation. The more you do this and make it a part of your day, the more you'll own your positive thoughts, the more you'll live them in everything you do, and the more you'll find the world changing around you.

Chapter Nine

Travel, Life, and the Times We Live In

"Only two things are infinite, the universe and human stupidity, and I'm not sure about the former."

— Albert Einstein

As you know, life does not stop while we're on our diet. Work continues, vacations continue, and most importantly—we need to continue. With that said, one of the funniest situations I faced while on my diet was going on a cruise to Mexico. With a few enhancements to the program, I found that I could survive the trip, enjoy myself, and not feel deprived. First off, I decided that I would take along enough products for the entire trip and follow the program 100%. I attended all the sit down meals, all the late night buffets, and all the meals in-between. I never cheated once and actually was never tempted. While I know that I did not follow the most orthodox approach to this situation, the following plan worked for me. First, I always made sure to drink all of my shakes and never put myself in a position where I would be hungry. At our dinner table, I let everyone know that I was dieting, but that they should enjoy their meals and that it didn't bother me.

To survive, I lived vicariously through my wife. She would mainly eat what I wanted to try. That way, I felt like I could enjoy the menu and see the food I wanted, but not eat it. I found that half the pleasure in eating out is the process of ordering. If I could still enjoy this process, but not eat, all was good. We would actually make a little bit of a game out of it. Before long, other people at the table were playing along too. In fact, people would ask me what I would order if I was eating and they would order it for me. When the food came, they would comment, "A fine choice," or "You blew that one." Anyway, it sounds silly, but it kept me happy, it kept everyone laughing, and more importantly—it kept me from eating. Breakfast and lunch were always the easiest meals to survive, but dinner always proved to be the hardest. To get through these situations, I wouldn't eat, but I would allow myself a couple of stiff drinks. I would typically start my dinner with an ice tea, and then have my supplement, followed by a Scotch, and then I would have a coffee while everyone was enjoying their dessert.

This worked fairly well and I found that as long as I could supplement my diet with a Scotch or Vodka on the rocks, I never really felt totally deprived. Martinis also work well, but hold the Olive. Yes, alcohol does have calories, but I can assure you that I would have far fewer calories by drinking, than by eating. I kept the drinks fairly simple…Scotch, Vodka, Gin, and didn't accompany them with any sweet mixes or soda. As an added measure, to burn off the extra liquid calories, we would always end the evening with some time in the disco. If things ever got tuff, I would reach for the old standby cigars…a temporary relief to keep my mouth busy when additional calories were not an option.

Yes, I was substituting one bad habit for another, but it worked. In any case, a few cigars weren't going to kill me and they definitely kept me from eating when I needed them most.

Dieting and Airport Security

A funny thing happened on my way to Las Vegas. Since I was dieting, I took along enough supplements to get me through the weekend. Since I didn't have a special package for them, and put some in my suitcase and others in my wife's suitcase. Everything was going great until we got to the security checkpoint. You would be amazed at how funny those little packets look when you view them through the security-screening monitor. It really looked like we were packing C4 or some other type of explosive. As a result, we were quickly pulled to the side of the line and surrounded by a team of security officers. Our bags were unpacked and the packets were put out on the table for all to see. As you can imagine, this caused a huge stir not only for the airport security but for any passengers that were standing around at the time. And as if that wasn't bad enough, I then had to explain that I was a fat guy (like that wasn't obvious) and that the packets were part of my program. Definitely not a fun situation, but we had to laugh a little bit about it when we were finally released. Of course, my wife then looked at me and said, "I can only imagine how they would have reacted if they had searched our bags last year and discovered your suitcase filled with emergency snack items." So true!

Dieting and Vegas Buffets

Prior to having kids, my wife and I were frequent visitors to Las Vegas and as a result, I often found myself following her around any number of different buffets. For someone who was on a diet, this always proved to be an especially difficult situation. Not necessarily from the perspective of wanting to eat or being tempted by the food, but from the experience of trying to explain to the cashier in the line that I wasn't going to be eating. Basically, before entering any of the buffets, you are first required to pass through a cashier that takes the money for everyone in your party, and then points you to a hostess who then takes you to a seat. Unfortunately, when you are a man that is over 100 pounds overweight, trying to explain to the cashier that you won't be eating can prove to be especially difficult. Of course, as you can imagine, this is especially embarrassing since you are doing it in front of a line of several hundred people waiting to eat. This situation proved to be so ridiculous that the only analogy I can provide is to say that it was similar to an alcoholic entering a liquor store with a straw and explaining to the cashier that they were only coming into the store to read the labels. As a result, I often just saved my breath and paid the $30-$50 entrance fee to be able to avoid the conversation, yet still sit with my wife as she enjoyed her dinner. Of course, on the plus side, I was able to enjoy all of the diet soda and coffee that I wanted. And as I continued to lose the weight, I did find that my explanation to the cashier become more and more believable. But it definitely required me to take off the first 50 pounds before anyone would even listen.

. . . .

Home Town Food Culture

On various business trips and vacations, I have noticed how people in different cities and countries have different eating customs. This is obviously no great revelation, but it's interesting when you think about how much harder dieting can be depending on where you live. For example, while on a trip through the South, I had the pleasure of eating some of the most amazing foods, but I rarely saw a salad bar, noticed fruit salad on the menu, or saw any references to calories or carbohydrates. Culturally speaking, the South was a difficult place to be on a diet. Obviously, the South isn't the only place in the world that faces a cultural clash with dieting, but it's a great example of how some places are more challenging then others. Of course, if a person took the time to look between the fried chicken and servings of grits, they would also discover that the South has some of the most amazing seafood and vegetables available in the country. As you can see, regardless of where we live and the local delicacies, we all have choices. We all have the power to seek out the best foods around us and make the best choices for ourselves.

Personal Ingredient 9: Defeating the Pirates

Often the results of our weight loss threaten to change the balance of power in our relationships around us. Unfortunately, some family and friends want you to stay the way you are. And, in changing, you are in effect threatening their comfort levels. Amazingly, the group that feels this way might not even be aware of their feelings. But as you progress in changing your life, they'll start to act like saboteurs towards your success. To help you defeat these pirates and learn how to assert your rights, your ninth personal ingredient provides you with the ability to create a support system that will ensure your success.

In examining your own life, it is critical to determine if you are surrounded by pirates. To do this, ask yourself if you have people in your life that do the following things:

- Invite you to dinner or lunch even though they know you are on a diet.
- Constantly bring you foods to snack on during the day.
- Talk about all of your favorite foods.

- Talk about how diets never work or how you'll never succeed.
- Remind you of past failures.
- Try to convince you to cheat on your diet.
- Purposely put you into hard situations that they know will be difficult for you.

Now, if you are seeing that you have pirates in your life, it's essential to learn how to assert your rights. If it's not something that you are used to, it can be scary, but never forget that you are protecting yourself when doing this and that it's crucial to handle pirates directly. So, to assert yourself, use the word "I" to get your message across. You want to tell the person how the behavior makes you feel and what you want. This might sound confrontational, but remember, most pirates don't realize what they are doing. Keep in mind, the more upfront you can be with the pirate about how their behavior impacts you and how it makes you feel, the more responsive they'll be.

By approaching the pirates in your life, you will make your relationship with them become stronger. The truth is that the actions of these people would mean nothing if they didn't influence you in some way. So, by talking to them about what it is they are doing, you are also saying that they are important people to you and that you need their assistance. Amazingly, you'll find that in doing this, you'll be converting the pirates in your life into the people that become your biggest supporters. As you can probably guess, dealing with pirates is never easy, but as you create your New Lifestyle, asserting your own needs is a critical step.

Chapter Ten

Putting In Your Time

"Do, or do not. There is no 'try'."
— Yoda

The journey that you started is not an easy one, and as you have discovered, it will test your willpower, discipline, and make you face issues that you probably never even knew existed. I know most people think that they are just going on a diet, but as they progress, they soon understand that to be successful they must overcome many lifelong behaviors. So now consider yourself a veteran....

You didn't fail!!!! What you did was allow yourself to learn more about areas of your life that you need to work on. I know it may sound odd, but what many people consider to be failures are life lessons. Meaning, you fell off of your diet for a reason. Something happened in your life that made you go back to old eating habits. This is good news!!! Now you have something to look back on and contemplate.

Think about what you have just been through...Think about what caused you to fall off the diet...Think about the events in your life and the things that you were facing...And I can assure you that the secret to your long-term success is awaiting you. If you can determine what happened, you can move forward with the knowledge to recognize those trigger situations in the future. For many of us (especially me!!), I had to repeat this process several times. I had a number of issues to overcome and it was not easy. I fell down several times before I found the courage to move ahead. Each time that I fell, I knew that I was learning and growing as an individual, so I could finally provide myself with the long-term skills needed for true weight loss success and maintenance.

. . . .

Success is Hanging In Your Closet

I was watching my wife clean her closet one night (it's a spectator sport in our house) and noticed something very funny. Basically, she was creating various piles throughout the bedroom; however, she kept a single pink skirt in the closet that was never moved. And, although I should have known better, I couldn't help myself from asking her the significance of the pink skirt.

To which she replied, "It's the one piece of clothing that I've always dreamed of fitting into again." Apparently, she wore it in high school and has always dreamed of wearing it again.

Now, what makes this funny is that my wife is someone that isn't overweight. So, I have a feeling that even in high school, this was a tight skirt (and that's all I want to know about it). But, in talking about this, I thought of the number of items that I had in my own closet that I used to measure my own success with. I know that I used to dream of wearing certain suits again and various shirts that had remained unworn for a number of years. Upon my reaching my goal weight, the suits and shirts did in fact fit again, and just putting on those clothes drove home the significance of my accomplishment. Yes, success was hanging in my closet.

Getting Better At Your Diet

During the process of losing weight, I always tried to be as diligent as I could at getting better. Meaning, I always tried to ask myself if I could be doing anything better, including being more consistent, drinking more water, increasing my workouts, or getting enough sleep. To me, the art of perfecting my diet was an ongoing process, but the following were just a few of my success strategies:

- I always kept my diet supplies in a box in the backseat of my wife's car and my car. This way, if we were ever driving around and found ourselves too far from home for my program meal, I would have one close at hand.
- I kept a good supply of items for my diet at work, not only by my desk, but also in the community fridge.

This also means keeping water, soda, and other supplements close at hand. Basically, the better you become at having your diet products and other items close at hand, the better you'll become at never having to skip a meal or feel tempted to cheat.

As I mentioned before, this was really not something that I valued or became very good at until I had almost reached the end of my diet, but if I had been better at this early on, I have no doubt that my success would have been increased.

Don't Postpone Joy

Don't postpone joy!! This simple statement is so true! When you are on your diet you are working towards creating a new you. Your life is going to change in some incredible ways when you reach your goal weight.

Start getting excited. Be excited for what you are doing and where you are going. While you are definitely changing your life, you are also enhancing it. So, be joyful of the experience and the opportunity and know that even the process is part of the goal. Remember, life is too short, so be happy and enjoy it. Smile while you are sipping or eating that special meal, and laugh while you are following your program, and don't forget to enjoy yourself along the way.

The Mirror and Your Mind

Dieting takes discipline and hard work. While the results are definitely worth it, for those with a significant amount of weight to lose, you have to put in the time. Yes, people can be motivated to do anything for a couple of weeks, but to be able to stick with something for several months' takes dedication and the drive to want to change your life. And as anyone that has done it will tell you, our reflection does not mirror what we see in our own mind. The more you live a healthy lifestyle, exercise, and eat correctly, the better you will feel about yourself. However, for someone with a considerable amount of weight to lose, changing our mental image into a new physical one can be a little frustrating.

During this transition period, view yourself like a large piece of clay. And you are the sculptor! But instead of using a hammer and chisel to create your sculpture, you are chiseling away with your diet, and are creating the new you in front of your own eyes.

Time Machine Syndrome

Dieting requires total focus and commitment for your future. But don't lose touch with the present.

I know that in a perfect world, we'd all like to step into a time machine large, and step out slim and healthy. Since time machines don't exist, one of the biggest traps anyone can fall into is not living life in the present. Yes, you should keep your eyes on the prize, but don't forget to start living now too.

I know for myself, I said things like…When I reach my goal weight, I'm going to...

- Look up old friends.
- Ask for a promotion.
- Go dancing.
- Do something nice for myself.
- Go on vacation.
- Start putting your needs first.

It's great to have goals...but don't forget to have some fun and live life now. Take it from me...I made the mistake of putting many life things on hold while I lost my weight. Reaching my goal weight was fantastic, but I could have done a much better job of living my life at the time.

Time Passes With or Without You

If you are feeling down or blue about the overwhelming task ahead of you and worried how long it is going to take you to lose all of your weight, I have something for you to consider. Think about it, the next 6 months of your life are going to continue whether you are on a diet or not. In truth, if you consider the fact that you are unable to stop time, the only real power you have is how you utilize it. So, by taking the position that you will just follow a program, not fight it, and let time take care of the rest, ultimately success can be yours. Now, if you go one step further and also strive to address your behavior and eating issues, the next 6 months of your life can be the biggest life altering time in your life. So, get psyched!!!

. . . .

Personal Ingredient 10: Becoming Aware

Not surprisingly, most dieters feel like eating when they either see food or are put in certain situations. So, your tenth personal ingredient focuses on being aware of the world around you.

The next time you are in the grocery store, take a moment and look at the products on the shelves from the perspective of how visual they are. This is something that you may have always realized, but not something that you specifically focused on. What you are going to see are some highly visible labels. Even worse, when you turn on the television, the visual temptations from the commercials can be unbearable. Visual cues work to stimulate your food issues. As someone taking back control of their life, it's vital that you become aware of these visual cues and gain control over your responses to them.

Therefore, with the understanding of what is going on around you, review the following techniques for overcoming these situations and see which ones will work best in your life:

Plan Ahead: You should already be doing this, but the simple process of planning your daily diet and sticking to the list will greatly help to control your being subjected to sights and smells of foods that are not on your menu. For many people, merely having a plan and sticking with it is 99% of the reason they succeed.

Don't Follow the Maze: Never go into a grocery store without a list. Even if you are just shopping for a few items, take the list to the store with you. Also, many of us are not aware of the intentional merchandising of the store. Meaning, every turn, every end cap, and every aisle has been well thought out with visual cues to make you want to buy the products. To avoid falling into this trap, DON'T FOLLOW THE MAZE!! Do not walk up and down each aisle and don't aimlessly follow the same path as everyone else. When you shop for food, do it with intention. Know what you are buying and go directly to those items. This doesn't mean that you can't enjoy your food shopping experience; it just means that you are going to be more aware of what is going on around you.

Hit the Mute Button: The visual cues on television commercials are probably the most powerful ones on the face of the earth. So, when watching TV, be especially careful when the commercials come on. Ideally, you'll choose to get rid of your TV. But let's face it, since we don't want to miss "Desperate Housewives" or" Lost," commercials are a necessary evil. To get through them, practice using your mute button. Basically, when you can't hear the commercial, you won't be tempted to watch it. And nothing will take your mind off of the commercials better then a good book, magazine, or by moving your body by folding laundry, doing leg lifts, or even crunches. Regardless, when the commercials come on, hit the mute button and focus your mind on other things.

Two of the most powerful cues are time of day and location. For example, since we were children, we have been taught that we eat at certain times of the day. Not only is this relevant in school, but also in the workplace. So, the next time everyone is rushing out for lunch, think about whether you are really hungry or not. You can begin to identify various situations where people eat because it's customary, but not necessary. The following are a few examples:

- Eating at the Movies

- Eating During Coffee Breaks
- Eating While Watching a Sporting Event
- Eating at an Amusement Park

Take a moment and think of things that you do today and how you can immediately change them.

Now it's time to gain control over the situations around you. As you progress on your journey, whether you are at the grocery store, watching television, or in a situation where people are expected to eat for no reason at all, make it a point to be aware of what is going on around you. Be conscious of what you are being subjected to and be aware of how you are responding to it. The more aware you become, the more power you will have in taking back control of your life. Just remember, although this may seem hard to do, and a little scary at first, it is a critical step to creating your New Lifestyle. Essentially, in doing this, you are giving yourself the personal ingredient to grant yourself the freedom to control when you eat, and the reasons behind it.

Chapter Eleven

Don't Fear Success, Embrace It

Victory is sweetest when you've known defeat.
— Malcolm Forbes

As anyone who has dieted knows, it's not uncommon to go on a diet with the belief that you are doing it for a set amount of time with the goal of losing a certain amount of weight. The very nature of this approach does not imply long-term change, but only change for a brief period of time. Not surprisingly, when people take this approach, they achieve success, but soon find themselves putting the weight back on. In simply being aware of this, it can allow you to appreciate the power of developing new behaviors and the impacts that they will have on your long term success.

Unfortunately, for many people that lose weight and don't develop new behaviors they often suffer from what I call "Post Diet Amnesia." Meaning, while they recognize the experience they just had and appreciate the results, they quickly take their success for granted. They forget what it's like to be overweight and how it made them feel. In many cases, they completely block out any thoughts of the person that they once were.

Anyone that has been on a diet and lost weight, only to find they're putting it back on, suffers from some degree of diet amnesia. By being aware, you can start to think about how you want to view yourself in the future. Not only the new you, but also the old you. I know for myself, while I love my new body and how I have continued to develop it over the years; I try never to forget where I started. In fact, in many ways, I look at my experience of being overweight as something that makes me special. The experience and process of change is something that I will never take for granted. In fact, I keep pictures up around the house of when I was larger. So, if I ever find myself getting too cocky, the reflection of my former self is never far away.

As you progress, it's important to enjoy the journey, celebrate who you are, and be at peace with where you came from. Don't hide the past, embrace it and make it a key part of your future. In doing so, you'll not only learn to better appreciate the new you and your success, but more importantly, never allow yourself to take it for granted.

Fear of Success

Fear of the unknown is such a powerful thing that I often think it's the leading cause of people not reaching their goal weight. For many people, the thought of reaching their goal weight can bring much excitement and it can also bring fear of new expectations. A fear of having to keep the weight off, a fear of sticking with a new lifestyle, a fear of having to set new goals, or simply a fear of being vulnerable to the watchful eyes of others.

The classic case of this is the large person that is hiding emotionally behind their weight. While they are excited about losing the weight, the very thought of becoming attractive and approachable can be powerful enough to make them stay heavy. While this is just an example, it goes to show how powerful our fears can be. In fact, the following is what I consider to be the top fears for losing weight and being successful on a diet:

Fear of Lost Identity: Many people remain overweight because it's a big part of their identity and how they see themselves in the world. They are known as a large person and they approach everything in life from this perspective. For many, losing the weight and no longer being big can often mean losing their identity. Frequently, you see people that fit this profile; they wear oversize clothes trying to hide their new identity.

Fear of Family: Many people are afraid of success, due to family dynamics. For instance, people that come from households where all the family members are large can often be seen as a traitor to the family. In fact, sometimes the pressure to remain large can be so intense, that the dieter feels incredible force to forgo the diet, and some family members may try to sabotage the dieter.

Fear of Friendships: Many people are afraid of success because of what it will do to their friendships. For me, I had a large number of friends that were really only eating buddies. When I went on my diet, I quickly found that I didn't have very much in common with these buddies anymore. I also discovered that many of them were resentful of my success. As you can see, the fear of losing friends can be a serious deterrent.

Fear of Emotions: People are afraid of success for social and emotional reasons as well. For many, being large isn't just a symptom of eating too much, but is also a mask from the outside world. This is especially true for people that have been abused or been through terrible relationships. Often, instead of moving forward, people will shield themselves by putting weight on and creating a barrier from contact or social situations that can cause them hurt or pain.

Fear of Excuses: And last but not least...my personal favorite. People are fearful of success, because they don't want to lose the excuse of being overweight. This may sound funny, but for many people, life's issues and problems are often blamed on the fact that they are overweight.

These are the people that say things like, "I would have gotten that job if I was thin," or "I don't make enough money because I'm overweight," or "No one asks me out, because of my weight issues." Sure, the world is a harsh place, but for many people, having a weight issue is a convenient place to fix the blame for all of the bad things that happen to them. Unfortunately, these people often have the greatest fear of losing the weight. Ultimately these dieters must face the issue of whether their problems are weight or personality related.

No matter whom you are, losing weight can be a very scary experience. Dieting opens us up to new situations that we may or may not be ready to handle. But never lose sight of the fact that life is an adventure and worth living to its fullest. And, as scary as being successful may seem, do your best to face the issues head-on and don't let anything stop you from achieving your fullest potential.

. . . .

Why Some People Succeed Where Others Fail

While inspiration and motivation are great, they mean nothing without the right attitude. Many approach their diet from a perspective of being denied food or as an inconvenience to their life. In doing this, people will often make the mistake of viewing their program as a temporary change and thinking that at some point they will be "going off" their diet. Not surprisingly, when people have a short-term mindset, the results are also going to be short-term.

For those who might find themselves struggling and looking back on an endless lifetime of dieting and failure, I would strongly suggest that it's time to change the way you are thinking. For example, instead of viewing your diet as a process that is denying you the foods that you enjoy or creating anguish in your life, try viewing it as the opportunity of a lifetime. Think about this.... Consider how fortunate you are to be in a position to do something about your weight and your overall health.

Ultimately, your diet is not denying you food, it's inching you closer each day to the new you. The new you looking in the mirror and thinking how wonderful you look, the new you that will enjoy shopping and wearing clothes again, and the new you that won't mind having your picture taken!!

Your diet is giving you the opportunity to have that, and so much more. You have an amazing and very exciting life ahead of you and your diet is just the first step for you to enjoy all of it.

Don't be Afraid to Fight for Your Success!

My wife and I were out and she was feeling a little hungry. However, we weren't in a place conducive to healthy eating. So, we looked around for something to eat and I kept rejecting her suggestions. I said that the choices that we had were not going to work for me. Of course, she got annoyed and urged me to just pick something. However, I held my ground and after 30 minutes of looking around, we found the perfect place for me. They offered a huge choice of salads, chicken, and other healthy items. As we sat down to eat, we both laughed a little. And, much to my surprise, she exclaimed, "Well, I had no idea that you wanted to eat something healthy." To which I replied, "It's not that I only want to eat something healthy right now, I always want to eat healthy."

. . . .

Personal Ingredient II: Protect Your Investment

Regardless of how well you are doing on your diet and the creation of your New Lifestyle, it's important to know that creating new behaviors just takes time. So, in the interim, it's imperative that you learn to use your twelfth ingredient to help you avoid relapses and protect your investment.

You probably won't be surprised to learn this, but most relapses occur when we first set ourselves up for failure. Meaning, we put ourselves into difficult situations. While the long-term goal may be to exist around food in any situation, it's important to stay away from high risk moments. This may sound extremely obvious, but the longer you are on your diet, the more challenges you'll face. For many, a difficult moment is being around certain foods. In fact, you might be surprised to learn that most people aren't at risk for relapse because of exposure to their favorite foods; risk of relapse is from exposure to stressful situations.

It's important to understand that temptation and old behaviors are never far away. In fact, they are a natural and necessary process to your overall evolution in the program. These are the things that were once important to you or ways of handling issues that you are now learning to overcome. It's natural that you will have struggles along the way. But it doesn't mean that you need to respond or fall victim to them. You just need to learn how to be self aware, so that you can recognize the situations as they occur.

Most relapses start by being in a difficult situation, without having a plan or strategy in place. So, to avoid finding yourself faced with a relapse, it's critical to understand your own triggers. What are your own difficult situations that could cause you to stray from your diet? Some examples include depression, loneliness, boredom, worry, stress, illness, injury. Think about this for yourself and become very aware of your own triggers. Having this knowledge is vital to keeping you out of trouble.

Now, having identified some of your own triggers, can you think of some ways that you will handle these situations? Some examples might include going to the gym and working out the stress or completely removing yourself from the situation.

Remember, the goal in creating your new lifestyle isn't to have you avoid high risk situations, but to develop the skills necessary so that you don't have to turn to food for comfort or support. But if a relapse does occur, it's important not to see the event as a moment of being out of control, but as a single isolated event that you can learn from.

Utilizing your new personal ingredients put the following set of actions into place with each temptation or hard situation that you face:

Stop and Walk: Whatever is happening, immediately stop what you are doing and leave the situation. Remember, it's better to walk away and regroup, rather than continue to make a bad situation worse.

Laugh and Smile: Remember, you can handle any situation with a sense of humor and no matter what you are faced with, never stop laughing and smiling along the way. Even if no one else around you understands, keep laughing.

Review and Renew: When faced with a hard situation, never forget to remind yourself of how far you have already come. In fact, take a moment and stroll down memory lane to remind yourself of the various successes that you have had along the way.

Then, think about the exciting changes and future ahead of you and renew your commitment to your New Lifestyle.

Get Physical: Nothing will take your mind off of a temptation better than hitting the gym and getting physical. So, when you find yourself in a hard situation, take advantage of the nervous energy and use it to burn some calories.

Remember, overcoming a hard situation or a temptation is nothing that simply happens by chance. It happens because you have a plan in place; you have already decided how you are going to act when the time comes. While this may require thinking in the beginning, the more you do it, the more it will become second nature.

Chapter Twelve

Life Beyond the Diet — New Goals and Motivations

"Quality is not an act, it is a habit."

— Aristotle

If you are anything like me, you can understand what I'm talking about when I say that I once was completely unable to quench my insatiable appetite. I can remember eating just for the sake of eating and only stopping when I felt totally ill. In fact, what was really sad was that I would often do this time and time again. Going to bed sometimes feeling like I was ready to pop, promising myself that this was the last time, only to find myself repeating the actions again the next day. I was on a vicious merry-go-round of eating and empty self-promises.

My behavior demonstrated a total lack of respect for food. I had my favorite foods, but it typically didn't matter what I ate. Cookies, ice cream, chips, pasta, crackers.... I was an equal opportunity offender when it came to overeating. And what seemed to matter most was not what I was eating, but how much I was eating. For me, it was all about quantity and feeling full which seemed to provide a level of comfort in my life.

Over the past several years, one of my major issues has been to learn how to create and manage a new relationship with food, to approach food from a different perspective of quality. To do this, I had to create a new lifestyle and a new way of thinking about food. So now I look at food from the perspective of taste and quality, vs. the perspective of quantity. Now my life is about savoring only the best and freshest foods. I'm choosing to celebrate life by only eating what I consider to be the best.

In doing this, it's critical to begin thinking in terms of living a healthy lifestyle. I know for me, whenever I hear anyone talk about living a healthy lifestyle it always brings about thoughts of eating nuts and berries and joining a hippie commune, but this is absolutely not what I'm talking about. I'm talking about breaking out of your old shell and thinking in terms of health from a food perspective, and in the way you live your life.

Allow me to give you an example...

As my former self, I used to love to eat out. In fact, I would come up with just about any excuse to frequent a new restaurant or stop for food. One could almost call it a hobby of mine...and from the fact that I was able to reach 321 pounds; I was obviously very good at it.

By losing the weight and really focusing on eating lean and healthy, something amazing happened. I discovered that all of the foods that I once loved didn't really taste that good to me any more. In fact, the foods that I truly started to crave were grilled salmon and chicken. Or grilled or roasted vegetables. Amazingly, the more I opened the door to healthy cooking and eating, the more that I realized what I had been missing. It's critical to get over the mindset of thinking that healthy foods taste bad. In fact, the more that you can approach clean cooking and eating from a taste and enjoyment perspective, the more excited you will become.

Food is only one part of the equation. As you are discovering, creating change in your life isn't just about what you are putting in your mouth. It's about the way you are living and how you are approaching life. You may have been like me and spent far too much time watching movies and enjoying life from the sidelines; if so, consider now to be your time to get in the game. See your program as your chance to get off the couch and not only go to the gym and get exercise, but to truly move around and participate in life. Then, as the snow begins to melt and the sun comes out more, make it an active thought to get out to the park, walk around in your downtown area, and participate in outdoor events and just live life!!!

You have given yourself the ultimate gift of life with this journey that you have started. Realize that this is a full contact sport and to win, you need to get in the game. So, truly embrace the way you eat or the way you will eat again, seek out those opportunities around you that will take you outside, and truly enjoy the new body and life that you are creating for yourself.

. . . .

Pretending to be a Thin Person

I know this probably sounds insane, but when I first lost my weight I had an overwhelming desire to pretend to be a thin person. Even though I physically looked like a thin person, I was still in the process of overcoming old behaviors and habits. And, as a result, I was still mentally a large person in a thin person's body. The fun part was that I was the only one who was aware of this.

For me, I never lost sight of the issues that I was facing and continued to put in significant training to overcome them. But at the time, I can see how thinking thin for a larger person can be a very dangerous thing. For example, when you are thin, it's very easy to convince yourself that you can eat whatever you want, that you can drink a coke or have an ice cream sundae and it won't have an impact on you, but of course that is not true.

Your goal is to truly think like a thin person, to approach each meal from a healthy perspective and view food as both a celebration of life and as fuel for energy. But this takes a lot of work. And unless you are ready, it can also lead to many temptations.

. . . .

Make a Vow to Never Forget

One of the things that always sucks about being overweight is that it's one of those few personal issues in life that you literally wear on your sleeve. Meaning, a person can have all sorts of issues in their life (drugs, alcohol, gambling, listening to polka music, etc.), but when they meet a stranger, the stranger does not see these things; when you are overweight, what you see is what you see.

And, to add insult to injury, our society has preconceived notions about what overweight people are like. I know for a fact that when I was heavy, I was treated differently at work and in social situations. When you lose the weight, you finally have an opportunity to speak for yourself instead of having people formulate a first impression based on looks alone.

This issue is still close to my heart. I know that I will never forget the way people acted towards me when I was larger. And, more importantly, I will never forget the people that showed me love and compassion either. I would not have the ability to truly empathize with those that might be wearing the same winter coat that I once wore and truly understand the shoes that they walk in.

Therefore, as you move forward with your journey and are able to break away from your own personal cocoon, definitely fly away and enjoy yourself, but never forget where you came from. It is often tempting to want to throw away the old photographs and start a new life with a new fit attitude. While nothing is wrong with looking ahead, make a vow to yourself that you will always lend an ear to someone and vow never to forget.

View Yourself like a Piece of Clay

Viewing yourself like a piece of clay may sound funny, but it's actually a very important thing to consider when coming to terms with creating your new body.

If you are anything like I was when I started the process of losing weight, the thought of shaping myself like a piece of clay was the last thing on my mind. In fact, when I looked in the mirror, the thought that came to my mind was definitely not clay, but something else. However, the more my body began to change through the diet, the more I came to the visualization that my body was like a piece of clay. I could slowly see changes. For me, it started with my face, then my chest, then my stomach...And, while the clay (my body) didn't change overnight, the image was shifting in front of me, and this is where the diet started to get exciting.

You'll always hear me talk about walking and getting your daily cardio, but I'm also a huge advocate of strength training. You know, hitting the gym and adding some lean muscle mass to your body. Many people are scared about doing this, but regardless of whether you have 50 or 250 pounds to lose, your goal should not be to look thin. Your goal should be to look fit! And as you lose the weight, nothing is more fun than seeing your body transform like a piece of clay from something that was once soft, to something that has muscle and definition. The bottom line is that the more lean muscle you have on your body, the more efficient your body is at burning calories. In other words, the more muscle you have, the more food you can eat! Obviously, our goal is not to become big eaters, but nothing feels better than knowing that the foods you are eating are being used efficiently. And having muscle is key to this!

So, why don't more people do strength training? Here are some of my favorite excuses and why they make no sense:

"I don't want to get big and bulky." Gaining muscle is not an easy thing to do. In fact, when you are going through the process of losing weight, it is extremely difficult to even put on 1-2 pounds of muscle over the course of several months. So, becoming big and bulky is simply not going to happen.

"I don't want to impact my weight loss by putting on muscle weight." Same answer as above. Yes, adding muscle to your body will impact your weight loss at some point, but only from a small perspective. Ultimately, it will actually help. As previously mentioned, when you add more muscle to your body, it actually allows you to burn more calories, thus increasing the efficiency of your weight loss.

"I'm too old to lift weights or go to a gym." It's never too late to begin a strength training program. The bottom line is that it increases muscle tone, balance, bone strength and stamina. Increased activity can help digestion; it can enhance bowel function and a person's sense of well-being and alertness. It can even improve sleep habits, and when done in pairs or groups, provide companionship. It will improve heart rate and cardiac function while helping to lower blood pressure and blood sugar.

"I'm bed-ridden." A bed-ridden person and those with physical restrictions can still exercise from either a sitting or lying position. Yes, maybe it's not what would be considered traditional strength training, but the following are some exercises geared towards someone that might be bed ridden:

a) Lift legs straight off the bed. Flex ankles and arms. b) Lift head off the pillow and turn from side to side. c) Breathe deeply several times, taking in as much air as possible each time. d) Squeeze a ball or sponge several times. e) Increase resistance by adding hand and ankle weights as you progress.

"I can't afford a gym membership." If you find yourself saying this, ask yourself how inmates in prison are able to get so big when they don't have access to weights? The answer is, they get creative! For example, those that are starting can begin doing standing bicep curls with cans of soup. Then, as you progress, hold bottles of water, then move up to gallon containers of water or juice. Sure, it's not the same as proper equipment, but you'll be amazed at how much progress you can make by getting a little creative with what you have around the house.

"I'll start lifting weights when I lose more weight. This way, I'll be able to see the muscle." Adding muscle to your body is not an easy process and it takes dedication and consistency. Sure, the rewards of how you look and feel are fantastic, but don't discount the work that is required. And knowing that it takes time to reshape your body, the best time to start is always right now!!

Remember, it's fantastic to lose the weight and feel better about yourself. But when you can also reveal a lean and fit body that has been hiding beneath your winter coat (or in my case, several winter coats) the feeling is amazing. Please accept my counsel on this one!! The process of losing weight and creating a new body is one of the most exciting things that you will ever do in your life. And with each pound that you lose, along with the process of revealing muscles on your body that you've never seen before, I can assure you that you'll never want to look back.

As I described above, as you reach your goal weight and have enjoyed the process of discovering new muscles and the look of your new body, you will want to continue the path of fitness that you have begun. While this entire concept may seem very foreign and distant, trust me, you'll be looking in the mirror before you know it...Looking not only at someone that has just reached their goal weight, but someone that has transformed their body with muscle and looks physically fit.

Creating a New View

One of the most amazing things about transforming yourself is the way your self-esteem and body image change. As you can guess, having positive self- esteem and body image is key to your weight management and long-term success.

As you progress on your journey, your overall self-esteem and body image are going to change dramatically. Regardless of where you started, it's impossible not to feel good about your results. However, while you will physically look different, you're mind will take a little bit longer to change. As anyone knows that has spent time in a larger person's body, breaking out of that shell and viewing yourself in a new light is a very scary process. On one hand, you have accomplished some amazing results, but on the other hand, you are still dealing with many of the same self-esteem and body images that you had before you lost the weight.

To allow you to prepare for this, it is time to begin the process of improving your self-esteem. To do this, take a deep breath, close your eyes, and imagine yourself at your goal weight. In doing this, describe to yourself how you look and how it makes you feel. Now, as you have this image in your mind, I have some wonderful news! If you can imagine the new you, then it can be created! So, as you progress on your journey, never let go of this mental image of yourself and use it as a constant reminder of what it is you are working towards.

As you break out of your old shell and begin to experience the new you, it can be a frightening experience. Many are faced with conflicting feelings on how they view themselves. Remember, changing from being an overweight person to being someone that is thin and healthy is more than just looks; it's also a state of mind. So, as you move forward in your journey, practice applying the following exercises in your life:

Mirror, Mirror, on the Wall: When no one else is around, stand in front of a mirror and look at yourself as if you have never done it before. View your reflection from the perspective of seeing something that you like. Completely block out any negative views and only allow yourself to see the positive. Ask the mirror, "Who is the fairest of them all?" And allow your reflection to be the answer.

Apologize to Your Body: Approach your body as though it were a good friend that you haven't spoken to in a long while. Apologize to your body for putting other priorities in your life ahead of it. Explain to your body that you are now making it a priority again and that you are looking forward to being good friends.

Give Yourself A High Five: As part of your exercise program, make it a point to acknowledge the physical improvements that you are seeing in the mirror. At least once a week, take a few minutes and look in the mirror. Then, give yourself a virtual high five for the areas that you are improving. And, as you do this, imagine the body that you are creating and how the process that you are going through is very exciting.

What is really exciting about the process that you are going through is that while your diet may be improving the way you look, you now have the unique opportunity to change the way you think about your body. Be comfortable in the amount of time that this process takes and continue to enjoy the ride. The journey is not just about losing the weight; it's about creating a New Lifestyle and a new way of thinking and viewing the world. And remember, the mirror is your friend!

Personal Ingredient 12: Keep It Off

The number one thing that most people worry about after successfully losing weight is the thought of putting it back on. Knowing this, it's extremely important to realize that transitioning and maintenance are also key aspects of your New Lifestyle. As a result, this personal ingredient focuses on a key strategy for keeping the weight off.

If you are concerned about the issue of putting the weight back on and how you will react if this happens, absolutely stop worrying—you now have a solution! Your solution is your personal red zone. Specifically, your personal red zone is 5-10 pounds above your goal weight. As you begin to transition and are actively maintaining your weight loss, use your personal red zone as your indicator for taking action. For example, if you find that you have put on 5-10 pounds, consider it a warning light that what you are doing is not working and that you have to get back on plan.

For most dieters, being successful at maintaining their weight loss is not an easy process and it takes a considerable amount of practice and learning. In fact, many people find that they have lost their weight in less time than learning to maintain their weight. With a personal red zone, you are allowing yourself to be accountable for your actions. See your personal red zone as a continuation of your learning process. As you progress into maintenance and transitioning, be comfortable with the fact that you are probably going to reach your personal red zone a number of times before you are able to find the proper balance in your diet.

Of course, if you find yourself reaching your personal red zone, the obvious question is...What action should I take? And, in considering this, the answer is very simple...You must get back to the basics! The important thing is that you don't miss a beat and that you immediately address the issue of the weight gain. Take immediate action and get yourself back on track by using the following components:

Take Control: Immediately put yourself back on your diet. This is especially important to consider in the beginning. Essentially, in returning to the basics, you can allow yourself to immediately get control of the situation and return yourself to your goal weight. Then, upon feeling comfortable, you can begin your transition strategy again. And just as we have done with all of the stepping stones, you'll be able to take what you have learned from the situation and be more aware of your triggers that caused you to reach your personal red zone.

Stop Eating Out: Many people find that when they are transitioning, they begin to eat out more often than they previously did. So, an immediate action that can be taken to gain control again is to stop eating out and get back into the kitchen. Remember, you'll always have the most success on your diet when you are preparing your food vs. someone doing it for you.

Keep A Diary: By the simple act of keeping a food journal, you can ensure that you are following the transition diet to the letter. In fact, you'll often find that mistakes are made not so much in what you are eating, but in how much you are eating. Keeping a diary allows you to take control and really analyze your success.

Avoid Hard Situations: Just because you now look different, it doesn't mean that you have overcome all of your issues. So, it's important to remember that many of your previous favorite restaurants or hangouts should still be avoided. In fact, eliminating your trouble spots could make all the difference to your success.

Exercise: Many people run into issues with gaining weight when they begin transitioning, because they have not made exercise a daily part of their lives. So, if you find yourself gaining weight, it's typically because of missed workouts. Remember, just 30 minutes of walking each day will do wonders for helping you to keep the weight off. If you can do even more, or incorporate weight training, you'll see even greater success.

Let's face it, life is always going to present situations where you are either going to be tempted to eat foods that you know aren't good for you or where you'll find yourself in social situations where food is all around you. But the good news is that you can absolutely learn to enjoy food. It just needs to come with a healthy dose of balance in your life of exercise and an understanding and appreciation of your own issues. In implementing these things, should you ever find yourself slipping, then immediately take charge and know that you have the means to take back control and get yourself back on track.

Chapter Thirteen

Final Thoughts....the Good News

> If you want happiness for an hour, take a nap. If you want happiness for a day, go fishing. If you want happiness for a year, inherit a fortune. If you want happiness for a lifetime, help somebody.
>
> — Chinese Proverb

Throughout this book you've been presented with a personal list of ingredients to live your life with and use to overcome challenges and behaviors associated with losing weight and keeping it off. To many, they would assume that this is where the journey ends. But the truth is that in order to overcome any behaviors and to create a new lifestyle, it takes time and practice. It requires a commitment to change your life and apply what you have learned in various situations and challenges that you face moving forward. So, treat your life as an adventure and consider yourself on your most exciting journey yet. Not only from the perspective of changing your appearance, outlook on life, and personal health—but in the many ways that "the new you" is going to impact those around you.

Be comfortable in knowing that life is never easy and that the behaviors you are overcoming are things that will always be with you at some level and show themselves when you least expect it.

However, with this information, you can now move forward knowing that as long as you don't turn your back on your past behaviors, you'll always be able to manage them. Ultimately, this is your biggest weapon to achieve long-term success. Never forget where you have come from and truly appreciate all that you accomplished. Amazingly, as you look back on the issues that you are overcoming, you'll truly learn to appreciate that the very issues that you had to work through are actually the things that made you special and unique. They were a part of forging who you are and the strengths and qualities that you bring to the world. And when you find that you are no longer burdened by these issues, you'll also find that the energy that they once required of you can be applied to new and exciting areas of your life. So, while you embrace the changes that you are creating in your life, also embrace the issues that you are leaving behind.

Moving forward, don't discount the act of helping others to follow in your own foot steps. I know for myself, when I started talking to other people and helping them to overcome the same challenges that I once faced, it truly made all the difference in my own success. Whether you are helping a friend, family member, co-worker, or a complete stranger, know that in helping others, you will not only be helping them to grow stronger, but you are truly helping yourself. So, as you progress forward, make a conscious effort and "Pay it Forward." Do this by being a beacon of success, not only in your physical transformation and your new outlook on life, but in each of your day-to-day decisions and actions.

Now, go forth and conquer!

Sincerely,

Hamilton Erridge

Chapter Fourteen

Contract for Success

Now that you've reached the end of the book, I would like to invite you to be part of something very special. On the wall of my office, I've dedicated a map to those that have read this book and committed themselves to the creation of their new lifestyle. I know from personal experience that it's not easy to make the decision to change your life, but I also know that when you truly make that decision, nothing can stop you. As a result, when you are ready to acknowledge your decision, take a moment to fill out the "Contract for Success" on page 165 and either mail or fax it to me. When I receive your contract, I'll very proudly place a pin on the map showing your home town and I'll have the knowledge that you have taken the lessons from this book and are now living them. Additionally, don't hesitate to send a note or a letter and let me know how you are doing. I love to hear from people and I look forward to hearing your story.

Contract for Success

I ______________________________(Insert Name) am 100% committed to my new lifestyle. I'm doing this for me and I understand that it's going to take sacrifice and hard work, but I'm worth it.

This is the place in time that I've chosen to do this. Not tomorrow, or next week, but right now. I'm committed to reaching my goal and nothing is going to stop me, not even myself. I'm going to live a different life and I know that it means dedication.

I know that if I don't start changing my life right now, the harder it will become. I'm making this promise to myself to succeed and nothing is going to stop me. Stand back world; I'm living my new lifestyle starting right now!!

Signature: ______________________________________

Name: ____

City: ______________________ State/Province: ________

Zip/Postal Country:____________

E-mail: ____

Mail: Hamilton Erridge
2415 San Ramon Valley Blvd. Suite 4-301
San Ramon, CA 94583 - USA

Fax: 925-687-2165